MW01490003

What Readers Are Saying About Vernette M. Carlson and *Accounting for The Civil War*

"A fascinating account of the American Civil War that uses a broad array of census data and other primary sources as a launching point."—*David Voelker, PhD, Professor of History , University of Wisconsin, Green Bay .*

Dr. Carlson provides a picture of 1860s America that can be lost in concentrating on the ideology, battles and generals of the Civil War. Here we see the human, economic and resource factors that are often missed by the nonprofessional student of American history. Her use of census data and the Harper's 1866 and 1868 study of the war reveal the great cost of the war beyond the loss of life. *Accounting for the Civil War* is most certainly not the usual United States history book. —*Mark Johnson, PhD*

The book provides insights into the development of significant differences between traditional labor-intensive agrarian states of the south and the northern states that were becoming quite industrialized. These differences were prominent in determining the destiny of the nation that would develop out of the existing states and states that would come out of the territories to the west. The factors that led to the war between the states had profound beginnings that are well substantiated in the book.—*William H. Anderson, PhD, Regional Chief Scientist (retired), National Capital Region, National Park Service.*

Also by Vernette M. Carlson M.D.

Preaching a Social Gospel; Eccentricities of the Shepherds
Forthcoming

ACCOUNTING FOR THE CIVIL WAR

NOT THE USUAL UNITED STATES HISTORY BOOK

Vernette M. Carlson, MD

Moonshine Cove Publishing, LLC

ISBN: 978-1-937327-149
Library of Congress Control Number: 2012951587

Also available in Kindle, Nook and ePub formats
Manufactured in the United States of America

Thanks to my husband, Brian, our three children, Bethany, Ben, Sarah and Noah, and to my office family for their love, support and encouragement. Most importantly, thanks to our God for placing these people in my life. Philippians 1:3-6

AUTHOR'S NOTE

This paragraph is a challenge to you to NOT open this book unless you want a different perspective on our American Civil War. No dates to remember, no specific battle diagrams, only overviews of the richness of antebellum and Civil War experiences and some of the most interesting, yet rarely seen illustrations from some of the most popular sources and artists of the era. These reflect struggles, creativity, heroics, lesser known biographies, and our heritage. Sacrifices, industry, geography, agriculture, and demographics are all ingredients in this unique history.

Open this book, if you want to travel back in time to a younger United, then fractured, non-united States. Likely, something will be of interest to you, even if traditional presentations of history have been boring or less than inspiring to you. It is my hope that this account will be shared with others and help to foster the development of new history fanatics.

Vernette M. Carlson, M.D.

CONTENTS

REPRODUCED ILLUSTRATIONS

Introduction - Decade of Decades

Ten years can be seen as eternally significant. Viewed in the perspective of history, a single decade can make or break the greatest of countries, empires or unions. In the United States, the singular decade of survival, leading to the manifest destiny of these *United States of America,* was the 1850s. Viewed as the ultimate watershed between the success of the Revolutionary War and the cataclysm of the Civil War, this ten year period was definitive in the disintegration of the newly formed United States. If this period of mounting stressors had not culminated in a winnable war for the Union, the modern United States would be very different from what it is today. Very likely the region to the north of the Mason Dixon line would have remained as these United States. Correspondingly the southern region under the Confederacy would have remained, and possibly thrived, as the Confederate States of America. If recognized as an independent nation in the year of the 7th Census in 1860, The Confederacy would have been the fourth richest country in the world. Unfortunately, within four years this area was devastated physically, emotionally, and financially.

By reviewing Census information, collected decennially, the evolution of the young United States may be viewed in a staccato pattern. Each Census becomes a still picture of the Country. When these static snapshots of the nation are visualized sequentially the census statistics become fluid, filled with motion, similar to a motion picture. Akin to little drawings with slight differences recorded on each page of a notebook and then rapidly flipped passed, the Censuses can be viewed as the individual pictures. Each of these frames, when combined, flow into a vivid moving picture of the United States.

Statistics derived through the most personal of interactions between individuals and representatives of the federal government are among the most accurate sources of historical data available to historians. While individual diaries, letters, and oral histories add richness to the historical record, these versions of history can be potentially more inaccurate or deceptive than that obtained in the Constitution mandated census efforts. While it is well known that individuals can lie to the federal government, early census takers were often in a relatively good position to detect gross misrepresentations in their neighbor's questionnaires.

Additionally, these census records can be complemented, personalized and, at times, corroborated, by examining biographies of some enumerated individuals. While these statistics and Census records are invaluable in viewing the big picture of this era, each scene requires the capture of images of individuals. These images are composed of verbal accounts and visual accounts, now known as the audio-visual record. The included speeches, quotes and stories are illuminated by illustrations from contemporary sources, where possible. Such sources as *Harper's Pictorial History of the Civil War* and *Frank Leslie's Illustrated History of the Civil War* are treasure troves of history which were meant to be shared.

Harper's Pictorial History of the Civil War was issued as a two volume set, with the first volume published in May of 1866. This temporal proximity to the close of the Civil War, reveals raw emotions and regional sentiments. In fact, the title of the volumes which used the term, "Civil War," was more sensitive to the South than the first line of the PREFACE of the 1866 volume. This compilation, by Alfred H. Guernsey and Henry M. Alden, began with a clear definition of purpose: "We have undertaken to write the History of the Great Rebellion in the United States. Our task was commenced during the agony of the great struggle, when no man could foretell its issue. We purposed at the outset to narrate events just as they occurred; to speak of living men as impartially as though they were dead; to praise no man unduly because he strove for the right, to malign no man because he strove for the wrong; to anticipated, as far as we might, the sure verdict of after ages upon events in which we felt the keenest personal interest."

We now can review these monumental volumes from the perspective "of after ages."

In addition, through the information available to these men and discussed in this book, the statement, "no man could foretell its issue," is strongly debatable. Regardless of our personal perspectives on the Civil War, whether justified and moral or illegal and immoral, Guernsey and Alden lived in the moment and at some point we must trust some historical documents to be accurate, or at least less inaccurate than others. Reflecting on their credibility, "We have based this History throughout upon authentic documents. We have made no statement which we have not believed to be true, and also substantiated by unquestioned evidence. We have drawn no deductions which we did not think warranted by the facts adduced."

Since the volumes were written in the North, with the PREFACE initialed by these authors and dated "May, 1866" in New York, entered by an "Act of Congress.. by Harper and Brothers, in the Clerk's Office of the District Court of the Southern District of New York," and published by McDonnell Bros., Chicago, Illinois, a Northern bias would have been impossible to totally avoid. The South was, unfortunately, in no condition to publish such massive works in this close proximity to the conclusion of actual outright warfare. With this knowledge, the issues published by Harper and Brothers are impressive. In addition this source states that, "If our work has advanced slowly, it has been because at each step new materials came to light which demanded careful examination. The close of the war gave us access to documents before unattainable, which we yet judged essential to the proper understanding of our subject. We knew before how the war had been waged against the Confederacy, but we knew only in part how it had been waged by the Confederacy."

This book was intended to build upon these primary sources and to emulate Harper's goal of issuing a "Pictorial History, in which the Illustrations were to form an integral part of the text." As the authors (and I) discovered, "We have wrought in common, each having access to all the materials, and consulting throughout upon the use to be made of them. We can now see clearly before us the labor which remains to be accomplished. We trust that within a few months, and within the compass of another volume similar to this, we shall be able to bring to a close the "History of the Great Rebellion in the United States."[1]

While the first volume contained 380 pages with detailed index, the second volume, not

---

[1] Harper's Pictorial History of the Civil War. Preface,

published until 1868, included an additional 456 pages. The first issue covered up to August 1862 and the next volume covered the remainder of the War. The second PREFACE documented that "The writing of this History has extended over a period of five years. It began while the conflict of arms was at the hottest, and before it had passed its doubtful period; it is now concluded nearly three years after the surrender of the rebel armies, but before the final stage of Reconstruction can be fairly said to have been inaugurated. It has been a work of great magnitude, covering as it does the events of seven years—and those seven the most important in our national history."

By 1868, the authors felt that "We have written exactly as we should have done if the interest of our readers depended upon the unadorned recital of facts. No pains have been spared—no expense of time or of study—in order to make this the fullest and most complete history of the Civil War which at this time is possible." Again it was stressed that Harper's was " not compiled from other histories, but have depended entirely upon the original materials furnished by documents of every description, military and political, no small proportion of which have never been published, but have been obtained from prominent actors on both sides of the contest. If we had hastened to submit our work to the public, such of this material, both published and unpublished, would have been lost to us, and our work would to that extent have lacked completeness and maturity."

Another major source for figures included in *Accounting for Civil War* is *Frank Leslie's Illustrated History of the Civil War,* edited by Louis Shepheard Moat and published by Mrs. Frank Leslie in New York.[2] Published initially in 1895, this 512 page edition covered, "The most important events of the conflict between the states graphically pictured. Stirring battle scenes and grand naval engagements, drawn by special artists on the spot. Portraits of principal participants, military and civil; famous forts: pathetic episodes, etc., etc. The whole forming an authentic pictorial history of the war... A concise history of the Civil War, being official data secured from the War records." The body of the volume itself is actually more concise than the text on this title page.

Both Harper's and Leslie's publications relied on the incredible engraving and drawing abilities of many artists of the era. Some that were regarded as well-known, according to Leslie's were "Becker, Crane, Beard, Schell, Lumley, Forbes, Nevill, Davis, Simons, Osborn, Wilcox, Weaver, Bosse, Newton, Rawson, Russell, Sartorious, Chamberlain."[3] In the antebellum and Civil War years, these unsung historians served as eyewitnesses who documented history in the years before technology allowed the widespread printing of photographs. By the 1895 publishing, it is also evident that some of the immediate postwar heated emotion had cooled. "Nothing recalls the past so forcibly as pictures of the scenes take at the time and on the very spot. A picture, too, is impartial. It cannot represent the success of the victors without representing the heroism of their opponents. It does justice to all sides, like Decoration Day, which North and South alike keep holy, and strengthens the bonds of sympathy between all true citizens."[4]

---

[2] Frank Leslie's Illustrated History of the Civil War. Title page. Mrs. Frank Leslie, Publisher. 1895.
[3] ibid
[4] Frank Leslie's Illustrated History of the Civil War. Introduction

The talents and inspiration of these authors and artists, editors, researchers and census takers, slaves and free, which live on in the public domain, deserve re-exploration in the 21st century. As stated by editors Guernsey and Alden, I, too, "have endeavored to anticipate the impartial verdict of the future. If we have failed in this regard, it has been an error of judgment rather than of feeling....Such has been the scheme of our work, such the materials upon which it has been based, and such the spirit with which it has been conducted. The main outlines of the struggle which we have here portrayed we are confident will stand the test applied by time and by the judgment of posterity."[5]

Figure 1 - Circa 1850 census taker

www.census.gov

---

[5] Harper's Preface. Volume 1. 1865.

Chapter One - An Accounting Must be Given

History repeats itself. Only by reflecting on past events and learning from the historical records can we hope to avoid prior mistakes and emulate prior successes. As philosopher, and 1872 immigrant to the United States from Spain, George Santayana wrote, "those who cannot remember the past are condemned to repeat it."[6] To avoid repeating the challenging and often tragic experiences of the first half of the 19th century, these years need to be remembered.. Fortunately, wise ancestors realized the need for record keeping:

"The senate then received the survey of the twelve colonies, presented by the censors of those colonies," so wrote Livy, in his twelfth book on the History of Rome.[7]

Tacitus further states that Augustus wrote in his own handwriting an accounting of his dominion. Over 2000 years later another handwritten census defined 13 colonies, recently renamed the United States of America. This "Statistical Account," was much more similar to the well documented efforts of Sir John Sinclair in his one man compendium, "Statistical Account of Scotland." In his twentieth volume he attempted to justify his monumental work. "Many people were at first surprised at my using the new words, statistics and statistical. The idea I annex to the term is an inquiry into the state of country for the purpose of ascertaining the quantum of happiness enjoyed by its inhabitants, and the means of its future improvement."[8]

It is with great irony that the "quantum of happiness" in many ways soon reflected so much unhappiness in the statistics of slave holding states, youthful mortality, and pending war. Sectional differences could be viewed as weaknesses, rather than strengths. In the eyes of most Americans in the early decades of independence, the new country bristled with opportunity, vast resources, most of which exceeded dreams of the founding generation. In order to better define the United States, a census similar to that of Scotland was to evolve. While originally designed by the US Constitution to function as a straight forward enumeration of population in order to appropriately represent the persons in Congress, a wide ranging accounting developed.

The inspiring "Account of Scotland contains the ancient and modern names of each parish, its history, extent, the nature of the soil and surface, extent and description of seacoast, lakes, rivers, islands, hills, rocks, caves, and woods, the climate, diseases, longevity, state of the church, manse, and glebe, the minerals, mineral springs, eminent men, antiquities, parochial boroughs

---

[6] George Santayana (1905) *Reason in Common Sense*, volume 1 of *The Life of Reason*

[7] Seventh Census of the United States, 1850, pg. 147

[8] Seventh Census of the U.S. pg 147

in the kingdom."[9] While it was acknowledged that the information in European statistical reviews "far exceeded ours," the goal of the U.S. Census was to present useful information in a user friendly format. Fascinatingly, it was admitted that the only volumes held in the Belgian royal library that did not fit on the selves were those of the Sixth Census. Ingloriously it was further disclosed that these books were stored on the floor beneath the shelves for the last several years. The "inconvenient shape of these volumes has led to their destruction, and almost entire extermination. Their extreme rarity, at this time, leads me to believe that they have, in many instances, unfortunately, been used as so much waste paper, not esteemed worth the room they occupied." How embarrassing. Immodestly, the introduction to the 1850 Census believed that, "Our materials are more varied and of better character than any nation has ever possessed; and shall it be said that, insensible of their value, we have not known how to render them useful?"[10]

This challenge has persisted since the most primeval enumerations. At least in terms of mere physical volume and print usage, the First Census of the United States contained only 56 pages, each measuring 8 by 5 inches. Despite being a weighty topic, this volume was the fulfillment of approximately 18 months of enumeration of the citizens of the young country. While the first counting began on the first Monday of August in 1790 and by law was to be completed within nine months, this proved a very insufficient period of time with which to receive, let alone to tabulate, even the most basic early forms. The United States population of this first accounting period was to be counted by United States Marshals or their assistants. In 1790, there were only 17 U.S. Marshals and approximately 650
designated assistants.

In addition, the returns were reviewed by the Marshals, before being sent to the President of the United States, who would then forward the aggregate census to the Secretary of State, who would then forward the results to the printing company.[11] With none of the analyses, percentages, and explanations which have become standard verbiage and digits of succeeding censuses, this early volume was compiled with no specific clerical staff. This compilation was formally entitled, "Return of the Whole Number of Persons within the Several Districts of the United States." It apparently was not a bestseller.

---

[9] Seventh Census of the U.S. pg 149

[10] US Seventh Census, pg 149

[11] Department of Commerce. Bureau of the Census. The Story of the Census, 1790-1916. US gov't printing office pg. 6

RETURN

of the

WHOLE NUMBER OF PERSONS

Within the

SEVERAL DISTRICTS

OF THE

𝔘𝔫𝔦𝔱𝔢𝔡 𝔖𝔱𝔞𝔱𝔢𝔰,

ACCORDING TO

"An Act providing for the enumeration of the Inhabitants

Of the United States;"

Passed March the first, seventeen hundred and ninety-one.

――――――――――――――――

WASHINGTON CITY:

PRINTED BY WILLIAM DOANE.
....
1802.

Figure 2 - First Census Cover

Adapted by author from US Department of Commerce. Bureau of the Census. The Story of the Census, 1790-1916. US gov't printing office, pg 6

SCHEDULE of the whole number of PERSONS within the Several Districts of the United States, taken according to "An Act providing for the Enumeration of the Inhabitants of the United States;" passed March the 1st, 1790.

DISTRICTS	Free white Males of sixteen years & upwards intending heads of families.	Free white Males under sixteen years.	Free white Females including heads of families.	All other free persons.	Slaves.	Total.
Vermont	22,435	22,328	40,505	255	16	85,539
New Hampshire	36,086	34,851	70,160	630	158	141,835
Maine	24,384	24,748	46,870	538	*	96,540
Massachusetts	95,453	87,289	190,582	5,463	*	378,787
Rhode Island	16,019	15,799	32,652	3,407	948	68,825
Connecticut	60,523	54,403	117,448	2,808	2,754	237,946
New York	83,77	78,122	152,320	4,654	21,324	340,120
New Jersey	45,251	41,416	83,287	2,762	11,423	184,139
Pennsylvania	110,788	105,948	206,363	6,537	3,737	434,373
Delaware	11,783	12,143	21,384	3,899	8,887	59,094
Maryland	55,915	51,339	101,395	8,043	103,036	319,728
Virginia	110,936	116,135	215,046	12,866	292,627	747,610
Kentucky	15,154	17,057	28,922	114	12,430	73,677
North Carolina	69,988	77,506	140,710	4,975	100,572	893,751
South Carolina	35,576	37,722	66,880	1,801	107,094	240,073
Georgia	35,103	14,044	25,739	398	29,264	82,548

Total   3,893,635

	Free white Males of twenty-one years and upwards, including heads of families.	Free males under twenty-one years of age.	Free white females, including heads of families.	All other persons.	Slaves	Total.
S. West Territory N. Do.	6,271	10,277	15,365	361	3,417	35,691

Figure 3 - US First census results. Adapted by author.

Few original volumes are known to exist. By 1916, two copies were in the possession of the Census Bureau and another was preserved in the Library of Congress.[12]

---

[12] Pg. 7

This earliest U.S. census effort listed the names of the heads of families and number of members in each family. These were listed by state of residence, with subdivisions into counties, and furthermore into city or town or smaller more specific units if possible. Even in the last decade of the 18th century, census takers faced, "The inhabitants, to whom an enumeration was a totally new idea, surmised that an increase of taxation might result, and were, therefore, in some cases reluctant to impart the information called for."[13]

This was not without credibility. Furthermore, even at this early time, sectional differences and competitions existed and the Federal government was viewed with some suspicions.

As with any relatively subjective information, basically forced into an objective format, the First Census is the best overall snapshot of the population enumeration of the young country. In addition, the lack of real roads, few bridges, vast distances to travel and very limited transportation choices, make the existing figures more appreciable. Although about 240,000 square miles were settled in 1790, this was less than 30% of the gross area of the country. It is, therefore, really realistic that many outliers were not visited, and, hence, not counted in the early censuses. Remarkably, some opposition was of a Biblical nature. "Moreover, in some quarters there was much opposition to the census, based on the Old Testament account of the disagreeable consequences resulting from the enumeration of the children of Israel."[14] This is a very interesting reason for resistance to being enumerated, especially when considering the sectional differences and brewing Civil War. The same numbers used to determine representation on a Federal level and strengthening a central government could be used to emphasize state differences and jealousies.

By the time of the next decennial census, more differences between states were disclosed, as age classifications became more detailed.[15] In another ten years, industrial statistics were included in the Third Census. Furthermore, the Fourth Census included occupational information, such as numbers for persons working in manufacturing, commerce, and agriculture. In addition, the Sixth Census further broke down the industrial efforts with the addition of mining, quarrying, and agricultural pursuits into the census of livestock and poultry. Apparently the animals were not all visited by Marshalls or assistants in person. This 1840 tallying also included educational statistics, such as illiteracy, school attendance, and numbers of the deaf and dumb, the insane and idiotic, and the blind. By this time the numbers, and comments relating to the statistics, were published in four volumes, containing 1,465 pages. These were two sets of "folio and two of quarto size."[16] This means bigger and heavier and potentially more divisive, by emphasizing differences between states and territories. Counting slaves and free individuals with personal details, along with mortality statistics, and with the most scientific details on products of industry and agriculture to date, the Seventh Census delved deeper into the strengths and weaknesses of each state and region.

---

[13] Pg. 9
[14] Pg .9
[15] Pg. 10
[16] Pg. 11

Classification of Inquiries	CENSUS OF –											1900 to 1909	1910 50 1916
	1790	1800	1810	1820	1830	1840	1850	1860	1870	1880	1890		
Population................	O	O	O	O	O	O	O	O	O	O	O	O	O
Occupations............	...	...	...	O	...	O	O	O	O	O	O	O	O
Mortality..............	...	...	...	...	...	...	O	O	O	O	O	O	O
Indians................	...	...	...	...	...	...	...	...	...	...	O	...	O
Deaf and blind.........	...	...	...	...	O	O	O	O	O	O	O	O	O
Insane.................	...	...	...	...	...	O	O	O	O	O	O	O	O
Paupers................	...	...	...	...	...	...	O	O	O	O	O	O	O
Prisoners..............	...	...	...	...	...	...	O	O	O	O	O	O	O
Benevolent Insitutions..........	...	...	...	...	...	...	...	...	...	...	...	O	O
Religious bodies.......	...	...	...	...	...	...	O	O	O	...	O	O	O
Marriage and Divorce............	...	...	...	...	...	...	...	...	...	...	...	O	O
Manufactures..........	...	...	O	O	...	O	O	O	O	O	O	O	O
Mines and Quarries..	...	...	O	...	...	O	O	O	O	O	O	O	O
Agriculture............	...	...	...	...	...	O	O	O	O	O	O	O	O
Irrigation............	...	...	...	...	...	...	...	...	...	...	O	O	O
Fisheries..............	...	...	...	...	...	O	O	O	O	O	O	O	...
Forest Products........	...	...	...	...	...	O	...	...	...	O	...	O	O
Wealth, Debt, and Taxation............	...	...	...	...	...	...	O	O	O	O	O	O	O
Transportation by Water..............	...	...	...	...	...	...	O	O	...	O	O	O	...
Telegraphs and Telephones.........	...	...	...	...	...	...	O	...	...	O	...	O	O
Cotton.................	...	...	...	...	...	...	...	...	...	O	...	O	O
Insurance..............	...	...	...	...	...	...	...	...	...	O	O	...	...
Cities.................	...	...	...	...	...	...	...	...	...	O	O	O	O
Street and Electric Railways............	...	...	...	...	...	...	...	...	...	...	...	O	O
Central Electric Light and Power Plants...	...	...	...	...	...	...	...	...	...	...	...	O	O
Federal Employees...	...	...	...	...	...	...	...	...	...	...	...	O	O
Tobacco Stocks.......	...	...	...	...	...	...	...	...	...	...	...	...	O

The Census Offic became a permanent bureau in 1902.

Figure 4 - Expansion of Details Included in the U.S. Census, Adapted by Author

One particular man realized the valuable contribution of the Census efforts to the nation. Unfortunately, he became personally involved in the Civil War, serving his native North as a Major General, later becoming the twentieth President of the United States. Reflecting his antebellum background as a teacher and lawyer, and his election to the United States House of Representatives in 1863, which cumulated in his resignation from the Union army, Garfield documented the importance of the census statistics to American destiny.

"The developments of statistics are causing history to be rewritten. Till recently, the historian studied nations in the aggregate, and gave us only the story of princes, dynasties, sieges, and battles. Of the people themselves—the great social body, with life, growth, forces, elements, and laws of its own—he told us nothing. Now, statistical inquiry leads him into hovels, homes, workshops, mines, fields, prisons, hospitals, and all other places where human nature displays its weakness and its strength. In these explorations he discovers the seeds of national growth and decay, and thus becomes the prophet of his generation.

The chief instrument of American statistics is the census, which should accomplish a twofold object. It should serve the country, by making a full and accurate exhibit of the elements of national life and strength; and it should serve the science of statistics by so exhibiting general results that they may be compared with similar data obtained by other nations. The census is indispensable to modern statesmanship."

Chapter Two - The Pursuit of Happiness Or Go West Young Man, Go West

Well known and documented by the Seventh and Eighth Censuses, the young United States was increasing in population on a phenomenal level. From an estimated tally in the Revolutionary War era, the struggling neonatal national populace was heralded by the triumphal statement, "We are three millions; one-fifth fighting men."[17] This ratio was essential to the military success of the Continental Army and would figure into the pending struggle between South and North. The growth of the Country was remarkably favorable to the northern states, and continued emigration, over this remarkable decade, was disproportionately prone to young, military aged men. Likewise, westward emigration was also dominated by young men. It was noted in the 1860 enumeration that, "Indeed, where a population has reached nearly its permanent condition, as in Europe, and the old States of America, one-fifth of the total population is still found to represent very nearly the number of males between the ages of eighteen and forty-five. But the emigrating ages are allied to the military ages; and in the newly settled States of the west, the proportion of 'fighting men' is accordingly greater, with partial exceptions, than in the Atlantic States. Thus, beginning at the east and proceeding westward, the number of white males from 18-45 is, in Maine, 19.5 per cent. of the whole white population; in New York, 20.8 per cent.; in Illinois, 22.1 per cent.; in Minnesota, 23.8; and in California, 47.1 per cent.' Disappointingly from the future Confederacy stand point, the 'similar proportion in Virginia is 18.7 per cent.; in South Carolina, 18.9; in Arkansas, 20.1; and in Texas, 21.9 per cent.'[18]

If the actual population numbers are examined, men in this age group total 1,064,193 in the states destined to anchor the Confederacy, another 413,370 were located in the soon to be border states of Kentucky and Missouri, and 5,210,695 were northerners. This essentially means that the south would be able to muster only about 20% of military aged men compared to the north. Foreign arrivals were continuously increasing this percentage in favor of the Union. For this age and gender group, 91,919 foreign immigrants entered the United States in the year ending June 1, 1861. In addition, a difference of 148,900 men was evident between those coming of 18 years of age in this year compared with those passing over the age of 45 years. It was recognized that 57,000 men of military age did expire during the same year, totaling about 1% of the group.[19]

As expected with the unresolved differences of opinion between northern and southern states, April 1850 was a particularly watershed year for the young democracy. Through the initiative of the United States Census Board, comprised of the Secretary of State, the Attorney

---

[17] US Eight Census Introduction, pg. xvii

[18] US Eighth Census, Population at the Military Ages, pg. xvii.

[19] US Eighth Census, pg. xvii

General and the Postmaster General, the demographics of the era may be followed, revealing the increasing strengths of the North, compared to the South. Growth was seen nearly universally, in practically every measured category. Besides the population increases, by the time of the seventh official census, initiated May 23,1850 and directed to the Secretary of the Interior by 1853, the country measured almost three million square miles. This made the young nation almost 3 times as large as France, Britain, Austria, Prussia, Spain, Portugal, Belgium, Holland, Denmark combined. In a more historical perspective, this area was approximately equal to that of the Roman Empire at its peak.

Interestingly, the first estimate of the United States' population was carried out in 1701 and published in *Holmes's American Annals*. Even this embryonic form of census cost over $1,000,000. Given the inaccuracies of the era, distances, and recording methods, the estimated total population of these colonies was 262,000. By 1749, the estimated census, with the addition of Georgia, showed a four-fold increase in total number. By 1775, the population ballooned, more than doubling in size. However, these early numbers were not differentiated by gender or race until the first true Census of 1790, which covered the current 17 states and territories of the time. Over the next 60 years, the census was conducted every ten years and covered 21 states and territories in 1800, 25 by 1810, 27 by 1820, 28 by 1830, 30 by 1840 and 36 in number by the year of 1850.

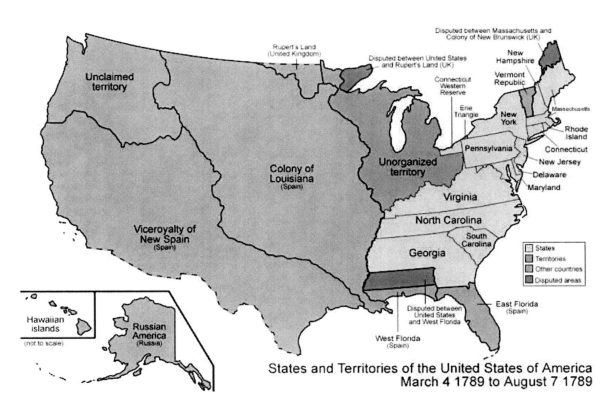

States and Territories of the United States of America
March 4 1789 to August 7 1789

http://commons.wikimedia.org/wiki/User:Golbez

Figure 5 - Organic act of 1789

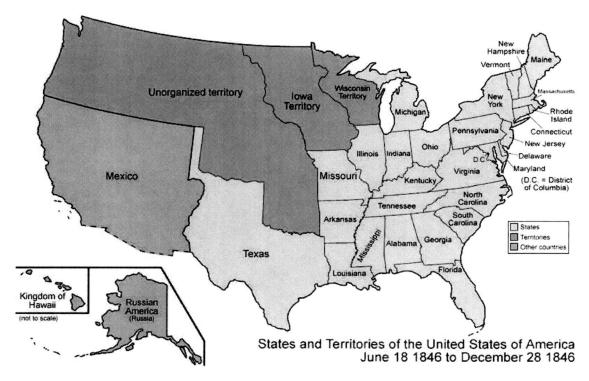

Figure 6 - Organic act of 1846

Figure 7 - Organic act of 1853

Census year	Total population	Land area in sq. miles	Population per sq. mile	Percent increase	Percent of total population in places of 8,000 or more
1870	38,558,371	2,973,965	13.0	22.6	20.9
1860	31,443,321	2,973,965	10.6	35.6	16.1
1850	23,191,876	2,944,337	7.9	35.9	12.5
1840	17,069,453	1,753,588	9.7	32.7	8.5
1830	12,866,020	1,753,588	7.3	33.5	6.7
1820	9,638,453	1,753,588	5.5	33.1	4.9
1810	7,239,881	1,685,865	4.3	36.4	4.9
1800	5,308,483	867,980	6.1	35.1	4.0
1790	3,929,214	867,980	4.5	....	3.3

Author, per census data

Figure 8 - Growth of the United states in Population and Area

In terms of the brewing sectional differences, these latter Census figures define the relational, proportional changes of the white populace, to the "free Colored" population, and "slave" numbers. Assuming general accuracy in these figures, the greatest proportional growth occurred in the slave population. From 1790 to the 1850 Census, an almost 21% increase was seen in this group. This contrasts with approximate 16% increase in the white population. Unfortunately, but not surprisingly, the free colored segment of the population increased to a lesser degree, with an approximate 13% increase.

From 1850 to 1860, the cumulative population increase was an incredible 35.4%, with nearly 4 million slaves. With a total population of 31,443,321, this reflects approximately 13% of the population owned by others. This reflected a very sizeable amount of capital for the southern states. Due to the predominately agricultural base of the south, slaveholding was viewed as a very favorable form of capital. Without cataclysmic upheaval in the southern economy, such as would occur in civil war, it was estimated that a slave would have 50% greater earning capacity in 1890. For the population in total, farmer was the most commonly listed occupation, making up almost 10% of those specified occupations. At 3.2%, farm laborers, those working for wages in agricultural settings, was the next most commonly listed occupation.

Notably, the first President of the United States was a dedicated farmer and kept thorough records regarding his agricultural pursuits at his plantation, Mount Vernon. As a first father of United States agricultural information, his personal records predate the inclusion of such specific data into the formal decennial censuses. In 1791, he fortunately surveyed fellow farmers in an "area extending roughly 250 miles from north to south and 100 miles from east to west which today lies in Maryland, Pennsylvania, Virginia, West Virginia, and the District of Columbia ".[20] Rather than attempting to visit these farms or plantations in person, Washington wrote to farmers to gain insight into successful farming techniques.

In this research, Washington requested details on specific types of crops planted, as well as produce yields, and values of livestock and land for personal reasons. Despite his position as United States President, he did not initiate a formal federally or legally mandated survey of agriculture. While the United States census gradually expanded to include similar questioning, a specific farming census was not initiated until 1839, upon an act of Congress. Interestingly, this program was conceived by Henry Ellsworth, the Commissioner of Patents for, "carrying out agricultural investigations, and procuring agricultural statistics."[21] The first such, "Census of Agriculture" was produced the following year and continued on a decennial schedule.

As this Census covered activity through-out the westerly expanding United States, cotton became the dominant export crop and, therefore, of greatest financial value during the antebellum years. Furthermore, this produce helped to define and delineate the most profitable agricultural areas and this information fertilized regional pride, pressing to the brink of War. As Senator James Hammond, from South Carolina claimed, "Without the firing of a gun, without drawing a sword, should they {Northerners} make war upon us {Southerners}, we could bring the whole world to our feet. What would happen if no cotton was furnished for three years? England would topple headlong and carry the whole civilized world with her. No, you dare not make war on cotton! No power on earth dares make war upon it. Cotton is King."[22]

---

[20] U.S. Department of Agriculture Statistical Services. Early History of Agricultural Statistics, July 2005, pg. 3
[21] USDA National Agricultural Statistics Service, pg 3.
[22] Pg. 4

Figure 9 - Southern Agrarian Culture at Montgomery, Alabama

Harper's Pictorial History of the Civil War, First Part, pg. 117

Chapter Three - Southern Agriculture, Less Diversity Leads to More Strife

As the southern states evolved economically, the region became centered on cotton production. With profits tied to the relatively extremely low labor costs secondary to slavery, moral objections to the "peculiar institution" were easily overcome by greed. The traditional planter class, dependent on the low cost of production, and strength of markets, sold chiefly to England or to the northern industrial states, where cotton was woven into materials and sold back to the states of origin. In fact, the southern states produced almost 75% of the world's raw cotton by 1860, making these fibers the most important cash crop to the future Confederate States. Even though other crops were of commercial interest, such as tobacco, indigo, rice, and other grains, slave labor was most profitably used in cotton production.

In addition, open farm land was most commercially valuable in the south. While the northern states benefited astronomically from the industrial revolution of the first half of the Nineteenth Century, the south remained agrarian for avaricious reasons. In addition, the northern states benefited from the migration of industrial, skilled laborers from Europe. While the United States experienced approximately a 35% increase in population documented in the census of 1850 versus 1860, the vast occurred in the north. While roughly half of the 1800 population resided in the South, by 1850, this equality ended, with only a third living in what would become the Confederate States.

The Northern immigrants expanded the rural population by 25%, but city dwellers increased by 25%. These immigrants spurred the development of commercially profitable industry in the North. Much of this nonagricultural profiteering was based on the massive natural resources located in these states. Deposits of coal and iron, in particular, made the Union States producers of weapons as well as plows. While the huge cotton output , estimated at 1 BILLION pounds per year, created plantations, as well as a planter class, and a very strong political base in the warmer states, cotton was predominantly processed in the north, or even overseas. This manufacturing ability turned the valuable bolls into even more valuable cloth of amazing variations, from finest chintz to heavy sail canvas. Unfortunately, the Confederacy was unable to clothe an army, or sail through a blockade without these goods, as ninety percent production of material was located outside the southern states.

As industry flourished in the Northern cities, the richness of Southern land decreased at a much more rapid rate. While initial agricultural efforts in the south enjoyed relatively rich soils and longer growing seasons, the same turf was planted repeatedly and repeatedly, which ultimately decreased soil arability. Unfortunately, production was affected and the concepts of crop rotation, erosion and economic diversification, which would have helped offset this depletion, were not well defined or practiced widely for many years to come. Some increased productivity was achieved by actual new land acquisition. Some was purchased. Some was acquired through the victory of the Mexican War of 1846 to 1848. When efforts to purchase western lands owned by Mexico failed, war ensued and young United States officers were tried under fire. Young Ulysses S. Grant and Robert E. Lee fought as brothers in arms.

Ultimately the War ended with the Treaty of Guadalupe Hidalgo. The huge expanse of land ceded to the U.S. totaled 525,000 square miles, totaling the largest land acquisition since the 1803 Louisiana Purchase from France. The area became parts of Colorado, Wyoming, New Mexico, Arizona, California, Nevada, and Utah. The South sought more states for slavery advancement.

Prior to the crisis brought on by this land addition, compromise had preserved the precarious balance between slave holding areas and free soil areas, where slave holding was illegal. The earliest "compromise" was that of 1820, entitled the Missouri Compromise. The Northwest Ordinance, enacted to control new territories north of the Ohio River was challenged in 1819. Formally entitled, An Ordinance for the Government of the Territory of the United States, North-West of the River Ohio, although also shortened in nomenclature to "Freedom Ordinance" or the super descriptive title of "The Ordinance of 1787", this act of the Congress of the Confederation of the United States created the Northwest Territory. This established the first territory of the young country. Affirmed on August 7, 1789, this territory was destined to form the free state of Ohio, admitted to the Union in 1803, leaving the remnant to be renamed the Indiana Territory. This early transaction provided territory that would be formed into the states of Indiana, Illinois, Michigan, Wisconsin, and about one third of Minnesota.

Very importantly, these new states were to be created once the population of 60,000 was reached within the proposed borders. While technical details leading to the admission of new states were mandated under the Enabling Act of 1802, more immediately and importantly was the fact that this law is an "organic act". This type of United States Congressional Act establishes jurisdiction over new land acquisition by allowing an agency or territorial government to oversee federal lands prior to statehood or more advanced governing. Similarly, the District of Columbia Organic Act of 1801 led to the permanent control of the incorporated District under the Congress of the United States.

Future Organic Acts led to the addition of New Mexico, Colorado, Arizona, and Hawaii as Territories, prior to statehood. Interestingly, this type of legislation has been instrumental to the addition of Puerto Rico, the Philippines, the Virgin Islands and Guam into the United States. Furthermore, the District of Columbia Organic Act of 1871 revised the Washington, DC government to create a single municipal government.

The Organic Act of most immediate importance to the Civil War, though, was the Organic Act for the establishment of the Territory of New Mexico, which was enclosed in the legislation of the Compromise of 1850.

While known for its influence on compromise, in terms of the expansion or restriction of slavery, the Act contributed to the future states of New Mexico, Arizona and Colorado. Initially the areas were to be governed by a Territorial Governor, with a three year term, appointed by Congress. After the population of "free male inhabitants of full age" reached a census of 5,000, application for a general assembly for a legislature could be made.

In 1819 Missouri met the criteria for admission to the United States. Unfortunately, this admission was desired as a slave state, although much of this area was destined to be free soil under the Northwest Ordinance, as it lay north of the Ohio River. Fortunately, the balance of the existing eleven slave-holding states to the eleven free states was maintained as Maine sought statehood as a free state, off- setting the admittance of Missouri as slave state. The right of each new state to determine whether slavery would be allowed became the essence of states' rights. While slavery is often cited as the inciting issue leading to South versus North, the underlying basis of Civil War centered on the right of each state to determine its own destiny. This was regardless of geographic location.

Even once hostility was underway and secession appeared to unify the Southern states, these specific states continued to, at times avariciously, look after their own interests. This was exemplified by Governor Vance of wartime North Carolina, in his attempts to look after the factories of his own State, "shared the suspicions of the factories, his wrath blazed up, and he seized the opportunity for exercising his favorite recreation of 'trying a tilt with the Confederate government." He further accused that the Quartermaster General of the Confederacy, Lawton, "was trying to break up the state's business with the factories in order to seize it all for his own department, and he demanded impetuously to know whether the confederate administration was fiving countenance to the nefarious scheme." Lawton of course, "denied the charge, and recounted the history of the troubles over the North Carolina factories, the growing scarcity of supplies available for the troops of other states, and the injustice and ill-consequences of the selfish policy followed by the state authorizes."[23] Compromise was necessary between states and whatever national government they recognized.

---

[23] Confederate Control of Manufacturing, Vol. viii, no. 3 ,pg. 243

Figure 10 - Fishing on the Levee of the Mississippi

Harper's Pictorial History of the Civil War, Second Part, pg. 431

Chapter Four - To Be, or Not To Be—a State, Slave or Free

The contentious legislation of compromise was headed by Henry Clay, known as the "Great Compromiser". The personification of the young republic, Clay represented Kentucky as both a Senator and as a Representative, serving as the eighth, tenth and thirteenth Speaker for the House of Representatives. In addition, he served as Secretary of State from 1825 to 1829. As a complex politician during several of the most perplexing years of the early Republic, Clay favored the War of 1812. Even though he was a planter, he helped develop industry by striving to increase tariffs. In addition, he supported strong Federal government and national banking. He also attempted to avoid inflammation of the slavery conflict by opposing the annexation of Texas.

Since new states were destined to enter the Union, very unlikely to enter two at a time, one slave and one free, Clay became legendary for communication skills and compromise. Particularly during 1820 and 1850, he became known as a member of the Great Triumvirate, accompanied by fellow legislators Daniel Webster and John C. Calhoun. While Clay and Webster, of Massachusetts, were known for anti-slavery positions, Calhoun, of South Carolina, became synonymous with pro-slavery rhetoric. Surprisingly, Henry Clay was a native of Virginia, the son of a Baptist minister, who died when Henry was 4 years old. In his father's estate, two slaves were passed down to this young son, and an additional eighteen slaves were specified as an inheritance for his widow. Compromise was likely in his upbringing, as he had eight biologically full siblings and seven half-siblings from his mother's remarriage.

Despite no formal legal education, Henry Clay worked under the Attorney General of Virginia, Robert Brooke. He was also influenced by George Wythe, the Chancellor of the Commonwealth of Virginia, and an educator of other great legal minds such as John Marshall and Thomas Jefferson. It was in marriage to Lucretia Hart of Lexington, Kentucky, that he became a Kentuckian. With his oratory skills, he became wealthy, a major landowner, and owner of as many as sixty slaves at one time.

In the murky antebellum politics and in the ironies that accounted for hostilities simmering for decades, the voice of compromise should not legally have been heard from Henry Clay. He was not of legal age to have been elected by the Kentucky legislature to his U.S. Senate seat until 3 months and 17 days into his term. If this irregularity had been noted and duly corrected, Civil War may well have been fought a decade earlier, and more likely won by the Confederacy. However, due to the "Immortal Trio", Clay, Calhoun and Webster, the Civil War became increasingly likely, although temporarily delayed.

Also, as a footnote to the antebellum ironies, Clay was the great compromiser but also uncompromising even under threat of death. After the completion of his first term in the Senate, finishing the term left vacant by the resignation of John Breckinridge when he was to become Attorney General of the United States, Clay was elected Speaker of the Kentucky

House of Representatives in 1807. By 1809, Clay introduced a patriotic resolution against members wearing British made broadcloth suits. He favored homespun suits and was only opposed by two members, one of whom was lawyer Humphrey Marshall. Known as an aristocrat with a "sarcastic tongue" and with a record of opposition to Clay, the two almost came to fisticuffs on the Assembly floor. The other wise compromising Clay challenged Marshall to a duel. Taking place in Shippingport, a settlement near Louisville, on a peninsula near the Falls of the Ohio, on January 9th, 1809, each man was given three turns to dispatch the other to their eternal reward. Fortunately for our history, Clay only superficially wounded Marshall below his chest while Marshall shot Clay in the thigh. Also, thankfully for our history, Clay was reappointed to the Senate the next year.

Only one year later, in 1811, Clay was chosen as Speaker of the House of Representatives on his first day of his first elected session in the House. Over the next decade and a half, the great compromiser developed the position of Speaker into one of power only second to that of the President. In that position he rallied support for the declaration of war against Great Britain, which became known as the War of 1812. After his position as leader of the War Hawks, he became a peace commissioner, helping negotiate and then signing the Treaty of Ghent, formally ending the war on December 24, 1814.

By 1820, the U. S. census totaled 7,861,927 whites, 238,156 free colored, and 1,538,038 slaves.

Figure 11 - John C. Calhoun   Figure 12 - Daniel Webster

Bioguide.congress.gov

Figure 13 - Humphrey Marshall

Bioguide.congress.gov

Figure 14 - Henry Clay

www.senate.gov

Chapter Five - To Free, or Not to Free? That is the Question.

Among those slaves enumerated in early censuses were those of the compromiser, Henry Clay. The most famous of which was Charlotte Dupuy, an African-American woman working in Washington, DC for her master, Henry Clay. In 1829, 17 years before the suit brought by Dred Scott for his freedom, Dupuy filed a freedom suit against the current Secretary of State, Henry Clay. She sought freedom for herself and for two of her children, basing her claim on a promise for freedom from her prior master.

Born into slavery in the household of Daniel Parker in Cambridge, Maryland, in about 1787, she was purchased by James Condon, a tailor, in Kentucky in 1805. There she married a young slave, named Aaron Dupuy, in about 1806. He was owned by Henry Clay and resided on his plantation in Lexington, Kentucky. In May 1806, Clay purchased Charlotte from Condon. Together the Dupuys parented two children. When Clay moved to Washington, DC in 1810, he rented the house originally built for the naval hero, Stephen Decatur, and brought his slaves with as servants. During his time in Washington, Charlotte contacted attorney Robert Beale, who filed a petition for freedom for Charlotte and her children, as she stated she had been promised freedom by her prior owner, Condon.

While awaiting the hearing of her case, she was allowed to stay in Washington, DC., residing at the famous Decatur House. Clay was allowed to remove her husband, Aaron, and their two children back to Kentucky, where her attorney was concerned that they would "be held as slaves for life." Charlotte also was necessarily assumed to be a free person of color in order to have her case heard, as slaves had no legal standing in judicial systems. Her claim for freedom was ultimately discounted by the Court as the agreement with Condon was not felt to be applicable to future ownership. For the 18 months during which she awaited the judgment, she earned wages while serving Martin Van Buren, Clay's successor. Clay won the case in 1830 and kept Charlotte and her daughter, Mary Ann, until 1840, continuing to enslave her son, Charles, for four more years. The great compromiser also arranged, through his agent, to have Charlotte held in prison in Alexandria, Virginia and then had her transported to Clay's daughter's and son-in-law's, Martin Duralde's, home in New Orleans. She remained enslaved for 10 more years.

Surprisingly, Clay maintained ownership of these slaves for decades after he had played an active part in the establishment of the American Colonization Society, formally The Society for the Colonization of Free People of Color of America. Presiding over the foundational meeting held at the Davis Hotel on December 21, 1816, Clay supported this Society which sought to return African-Americans to Africa. Joined by fellow luminaries such as James Monroe, Andrew Jackson, Daniel Webster, Francis Scott Key, John Randolph, Richard Bland Lee and Bushrod Washington, the group felt that blacks should be removed from America, preventing racial desegregation, as Clay stated, that "The God of Nature, by the differences of color and physical constitution, has decreed against it." The group helped to establish the colony of Liberia on the western coast of Africa as the site of African-American colonization.

Earlier efforts to return the free blacks to the continent of ethnic origin were supported by a Quaker, mixed race, wealthy, ship owner from abolitionist New England named Paul Cuffee. As a son of parents of African origin he had a very special relationship to the enslaved race. One of his parents was Ashanti, from the region of Ghana in Africa, while the other parent was American Indian of the Wampanoag nation from the area of southeastern Massachusetts. By the 1810 census the selected population which he hoped to return to Africa totaled 186,446 individuals. In 1811 and again in 1815-1816, he financed and transported freed African-Americans to Freetown, Sierra Leone. This endeavor in no way began to equal the volume of the slave export trade with Cuffee's last voyage returning only 38 American freedmen to this colony of Great Britain. By owning the ship, he had hopes of profiteering from the return trips, loaded with nonhuman goods. Other New Englanders, of abolitionist bent, often Quakers, joined with the famous Southerners to continue these emigration plans after the death of Cuffee in 1817. This rather unusual pairing of efforts was regarded as "repatriation." The abolitionists felt that the freedmen (and women) would be better off on the African Continent and the slaveholders felt less threatened if this segment of 186,446 was returned across the Atlantic Ocean.

By the 1820s, colonization efforts were redirected from the British ruled Sierra Leone to Liberia. This area of western Africa, bordering on the Atlantic Ocean, was first reached by Portuguese explorers, possibly as early as 1461. Initially found to be rich in flora known as melegueta pepper, the region was named "Costa da Pimenta", or Pepper Coast. The Dutch, in competitive exploration, founded a short-lived trading post at Grand Cape Mount in 1602. The area then remained unsettled by white men until the colonial power of Great Britain established trading posts on the same Coast in 1663. No formal colonization, though, was carried out until the 1821 arrival of the American freed blacks.

Land acquisition was gained through purchase and by military action. No greater an advocate for individual freedom than Thomas Jefferson proposed the removal of American freed slaves back to Africa. Noble gentleman James Monroe allowed his name to be donated to the capital city of Monrovia. The list of influential members of the Colonization Society included presidential grade leaders Monroe and Jackson, Bushrod Washington was known as the nephew of premier president, George Washington. This Washington became a Supreme Court Justice and owner of Uncle George's Mount Vernon, where he owned and sold slaves.

By the census of 1820, the freed black population had expanded to 238,156 persons. Simultaneously, the census of those still enslaved in the United States grew to over 1.5 million. Interestingly, this expansion occurred despite the ban on importation of African slaves into the United States since 1808. With approximately 13,000 of this "Free Colored" population transferred to the Liberian colony during the first two decades of its existence, the Colony was successful and became an independent country in 1847. Historically, although successful in birthing a new "free" country, the process of "repatriation" has been criticized as being racist and segregationist. While the distance does meet practically all definitions of segregation, the term, "racist," is debatable. At least the northern abolitionists would try to believe that the freed slaves would have a better life in the "old country." Meanwhile, the southerners found comfort in shipping off potential troublemakers. The wealthy slave owners were particularly sensitive to the concept that freedmen, particularly those able to read, write, and inspire others, could enflame other slaves to rebel.

Between the years of 1712 and 1831, at least seven major insurrections occurred in the American Colonies, soon to be the young United States. Surprisingly, the first memorable slave revolt occurred in New York City in 1712, in which 23 slaves killed nine whites and wounded six others. On the night of April sixth, a group of some 70 blacks ambushed white citizens in New York City. A fire was started in a building and as white men came to extinguish the flames, slaves sprang out and attacked and then escaped into the night. Suppression and revenge brought conviction and execution to 21 blacks. Of the initial 70 blacks arrested, six supposedly committed suicide rather than endure white justice. In contrast, 20 others were sentenced to be burned to death and another was sent to die by the middle age torture device known as the "breaking wheel" or "Catherine wheel." When considering the nature of planned execution, it is perhaps understandable why suicide could be considered merciful. When confronted with the torturous death, the term "coups de grace" or "blows of mercy", as sometimes meted out by French executioners, were used to abbreviate suffering by striking death blows to vital chest and abdominal areas while the victim was affixed to a large wooden wheel-like structure.

Not surprisingly, torture devices stemming from the Middle Ages did little to deter further slave rebellions. The next revolt of historical note was in September of 1739 in the area of the Stono River in South Carolina. This insurrection took place under "Cato," or "Jemmy," a literate, Catholic, Portuguese speaking slave, who led a group of slaves native to the Kingdom of Kongo. Kato and his followers, possibly warriors in their native Kongo, initially totaling about 20 men, expanded in number as they moved across colonial South Carolina. Nearing the Edisto River, between 22 and 25 whites had already been murdered by roughly 60 black men. The insurrecting band of slaves were then confronted by colonial militia, during which 20 white and 44 slaves were killed and a few surviving slaves were exported to the West Indies.

Ultimately, no uprising received the level of notoriety given to the efforts of Nat Turner in Southampton County, Virginia during August of 1831. Primarily known as Nat Turner's Rebellion or as the Southampton Insurrection, Turner led a group of slaves to murder between 55 and 65 white citizens. Amounting the greatest number of fatalities in any single slave rebellion in United States history, southern society responded with terror and organized local militias to enforce the submission of slaves. In retribution, the Commonwealth of Virginia executed 56 black slaves who were believed to have acted in the insurrection. Furthermore, local militias and rampant mob violence claimed additionally another 100-200 black souls. Legislation was enacted throughout the South, restricting the rights of blacks to assemble, to obtain an education, or to hold church services without a white minister in attendance.

In addition, slavery was further regulated through a ten year moratorium restricting the entry of slaves into South Carolina. Furthermore, the process of manumission, the freeing of slaves by their owner, was also affected. Sometimes this was by a will at the time of death of the master, or upon aging or disability of the slave, basically freeing them when useless for further profit of the master, or upon the owner no longer requiring the services of labor of the slave. Freeing 450 persons in Virginia, the "Deed of Gift" by Robert Carter III in 1791 was the greatest single act of manumission. These acts would at times be inspired by changing plantation crops to those which were less labor intensive or as reward for sexual relationships, or by religious teaching, most notably under the Quakers. In other less generous situations, the slave would be allowed to work elsewhere and purchase their freedom. However, due to the escalating threat imposed by the freed colored population, the South Carolina legislature forbade private manumissions and made government approval of such acts mandatory under the Negro Act of 1740.

The expanding free colored population continued to arouse fear in the white, southern population despite various legal and extralegal actions. Building upon the estimated 645,000 African slaves transported to North America, the black population expanded rapidly. In 1790, for instance, the slave census was recorded at 697,897, an increase of 77.6% in the previous decade. Over the same time frame, the "Free Colored" population underwent a 88.9% increase, totaling 59,466 by 1790. In comparison, the white population reached 3,172,464 in 1790, equaling a gross 72.6% over the previous decade. Considering demographic proportions alone, the white population felt increasingly threatened.

The support that radical abolitionists provided to both slaves and free black rebellions was another source of anxiety for southern white society. The most infamous abolitionist's action was in 1859 under the leadership of John Brown at Harpers Ferry, Virginia, now West Virginia. Unifying 16 white men with a fugitive slave, a freed slave, and three free blacks, Brown sought to take control of the Federal Government's arsenal at Harpers Ferry, which held 100,000 rifles and muskets. Desiring to fuel as major revolution in Virginia, Brown sought to capture firearms and more primitive pikes to supplement the 198 Sharps carbines, known as Breecher's Bibles, and 950 pikes already received in donations for his cause. Furthermore, John Brown hoped to have between 200 and 500 followers by the first night of action.

Surprisingly, John Brown's radicalized plans led him to reach out to the pillars of Northern abolitionist society, notably Frederick Douglass and Harriet Tubman. While Brown had hoped that Douglass would act as recruiting agent to plantation slaves, Douglass refused that, "an attack on the federal government would array the whole country against (sic) us" and that Brown, "will never get out alive." Tubman, the famous conductor of the underground railroad, born into slavery as Araminta Ross, in the early 1820s also declined Brown's invitation to participate due to illness.

Both Douglass and Tubman experienced slavery firsthand, as chattel, and attempted to save slaves without bloodshed. Unfortunately Douglass and Tubman had to gain freedom in more dramatic ways. They also spoke loudly and firmly and eloquently to achieve freedom for their fellow chattel.

Harriet Tubman was credited with saving more than 70 slaves by escorting them to freedom through the use of safe houses along the trace known to history as the Underground Railroad. She had escaped from a tragic life as a third generation slave. It is known that her maternal grandmother, Modesty, was transported on a slave ship and was reportedly from the Ashanti tribe of the area that is now Ghana. Harriet Tubman's parents held relatively high positions in the slave hierarchy. It is possible that her mother, Rit, worked as a cook for the Brodess family and may have been fathered by a white man. Likewise, her father worked on Thompson's plantation and supervised the timber aspect of the family's holdings. Sometime around 1808, Harriet Tubman's parents were married and had a documented nine children, with Harriet born as the fifth child.

Tubman likely inherited some of her independent spirit from her mother. Her mother's master , Edward Brodess, sold three of her daughters away from the plantation. She later hid her youngest son, Moses, ironically similarly to his Biblical name-sake, for a month when a slave trader from Georgia attempted to purchase him. When the trader and the master approached her home to remove her son, she reportedly threatened them, "You are after my son; but the first man that comes into my house, I will split his head open." They gave up on the sale. Later Harriet Tubman was hired out by Brodess to care for the baby of a woman, known to history as "Miss Susan." Her responsibility, at the age of five or six, was to keep the infant from crying as it awakened, but if she failed, she was whipped. As protection against the pain of this punishment, Tubman tried to wear additional layers of clothing, and at one time even ran away for five days. Unfortunately, severe treatment continued with even five whippings one morning before breakfast.

Tubman's body was further scarred by measles while working at another plantation for James Cook. There, even in her debilitated condition, her duties included running in area marshes checking muskrat traps. She, fortunately, was sent back to Brodess' plantation where she was nursed back to health by her mother. However, this healing though was tragically followed by return to work as a slave of lowest hierarchy. Logging, plowing, and running errands were the duties of her youth. While going for supplies to a dry goods store, Tubman attempted to avoid helping to restrain a runaway slave due for beating by his overseer. As the runaway slave escaped, the enraged overseer threw a two pound metal piece at him and missed, striking Tubman in the head. She felt that the blow, "broke my skull", leaving her unconscious for two days and with seizures. These left her "not worth a sixpence" and unable to be sold. Also, during this critical time of her life, she became firm in her Christian faith. Although she could not read the stories herself as a child, she was deeply influenced by verbal Biblical stories told to her by her mother. Also she began experiencing visions and dreams that she trusted to guide her life.

As an excellent representation of essentially all phases of slave life of her time, Tubman and her family experienced the heartache of slave sales, family separations, overseer mistreatment, religious fervor, near death illnesses and trauma, and even manumission. Tubman's father was freed through his former owner's will by 1840 and he remained in the service as a timber manager for his most recent owner. Similar manumission documents were found for Harriet's mother, which would also free her children. Unfortunately, these wishes were disregarded by her new master, who inherited the slaves.

Further demonstrating slave life, Harriett married John Tubman, a free black, in about 1844. Unfortunately, and in matriarchal domination, similar to cultural origin in African society, any children born to such a mixed union would be kept in bondage. If born in the reverse union, of free mother with slave father, the offspring would be free. Tubman had further illness in 1849 which made her resale by master, Brodess, very difficult. As an example of her faith, she prayed for her master to repent of his sin, in holding her and her family. When a sale was eminent, she instead prayed for the death of her master, and her master's death a week later left Tubman with regret for this prayer. Unfortunately, his widow did not honor the manumission either, and Harriet made a difficult decision to escape.

While working for Dr. Anthony Thompson, hired out by the widow, Eliza Brodess, Harriet joined two of her brothers in an escape. They had second thoughts and she was forced to return to slavery with them. Somewhat surprisingly, two weeks after their departure, Brodess contacted the Cambridge Democrat, posting a reward poster offering $100 for "each of the above named negroes, if taken out of the State, and $50 each if taken in the state. They must be lodged in Baltimore, Easton or Cambridge Jail, in Maryland." She left the next time without her brothers.

Tubman transmitted the news of her next escape in the form of a coded song, directed to her mother. This message was to be voiced by a slave friend, sounding similar to hymns of the time, "I'll meet you in the morning, I'm bound for the promised land." This freedom journey took her along a well-worn path through her home section of Maryland, through Delaware, and into Pennsylvania. Using the North Star and "conductor" assistance, she experienced the Underground Railroad firsthand, as a fugitive. At the time of crossing into free territory in Pennsylvania, she recalled, "When I found I had crossed that line, I looked at my hands to see if I was the same person. There was such a glory over everything. The sun came like gold through the trees, and over the fields, and I felt like I was in Heaven." She spent the next 11 years leading approximately 70 slaves to freedom in 13 trips daring trips into the north from the slaveholding south.

During this time, Tubman possibly stayed at the home of a fellow escaped slave, Frederick Douglass. Over the next few years, as both became increasingly famous for their abolitionist efforts, they also grew in admiration for each other. As Douglass wrote in tribute to Tubman for an 1868 biography of Harriet:

"You ask for what you do not need when you call upon me for a word of commendation. I need such words from you far more than you can need them from me, especially where your superior labors and devotion to the cause of the lately enslaved of our land are known as I know them. The difference between us is very marked. Most that I have done and suffered in the service of our cause has been in public, and I have received much encouragement at every step of the way. You, on the other hand, have labored in a private way. I have wrought in the day--- you in the night …The Midnight sky and the silent stars have been the witnesses of your devotion to freedom and of your heroism. Excepting John Brown--of sacred memory--I know of no one who has willingly encountered more Perils and hardships to serve our enslaved people than you have."

JOHN BROWN.

Figure 15 - Abolitionist John Brown-the spark which set the country ablaze

Harper's pg .12

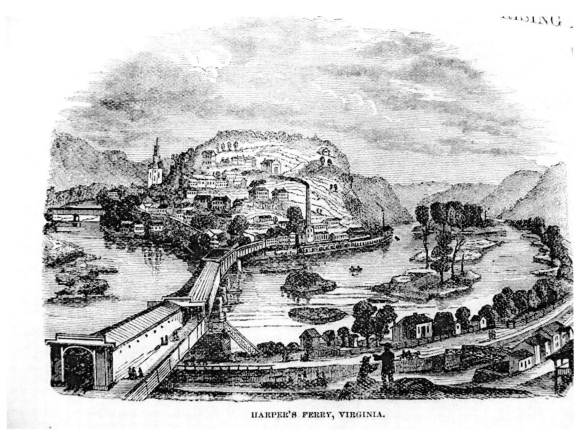

HARPER'S FERRY, VIRGINIA.

Figure 16 - Harper's Ferry, site of Federal Arsenal

Harper's pg. 81

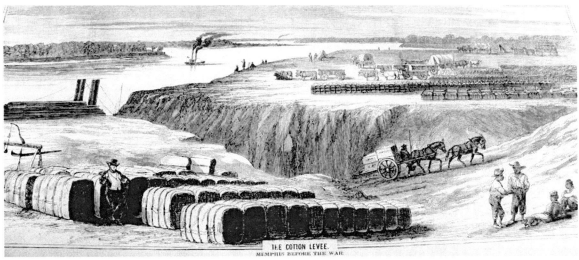

THE COTTON LEVEE.
MEMPHIS BEFORE THE WAR.

Figure 17 - Antebellum riches, Cotton on the Levee

Harper's pg. 304

Chapter Six - Speak Now, or Forever Hold Your Peace

As Frederick Douglass praised Brown in this writing, Tubman praised him to a friend, stating that Brown had, "done more in dying, than 100 men would in living." In living, both former slaves performed tremendous abolitionist activities, which defined their legacies. In contrast to Tubman, Douglass was known for his oratory and intelligence. These talents were particularly useful to fuel antislavery sentiment in the decisive decades prior to outright civil war.

Douglass was similar to Tubman, as both were born into slavery in Maryland. While Tubman's exact year of birth is uncertain, Douglass was born in February, 1818, likely a few years after Tubman. He suffered similar family tragedy, with his mother dying when he was about 7 years old, but he had been living with his maternal grandmother since he was an infant. His father's identity remains unknown to history. He was, likewise, moved from location to location, often from bad to worse conditions, during his informative years. Furthermore, he was severely mistreated at the hands of overseers and masters. In 1833, Douglass was punished by being transferred to work for a poor, white farmer with a reputation for "slave-breaking." After almost suffering a nervous breakdown, due to physical and emotional abuse and torture, Douglass rebelled against the farmer. Apparently the slave made a great impression on his surrogate master and the cruel farmer did not strike him again.

After two unsuccessful attempts at escape, Douglass met a free black woman in Baltimore, in 1837. She assisted him in attaining his freedom on September 3, 1838. He dressed in a sailor's uniform, traveled with identification papers supplied from a free black sailor, boarded a train, to the logical destination of Havre de Grace, Maryland, and then to New York. He described his arrival there in terms very similar to that of Tubman, "A new world had opened upon me" and "Anguish and grief, like darkness and rain, may be depicted; but gladness and joy, like the rainbow, defy the skill of pen or pencil."

On September 15th of 1838, he married the woman who made his escape possible. Moving to New Bedford, Massachusetts, a hot bed of abolitionist activity, Douglass discovered his ability of oration. Unlike Tubman, Douglass had learned to read and write as a child, aided by the kind wife of an early master. He overheard this man stating his opposition to slavery, in that if a slave became literate, he would become dissatisfied and want freedom. This further inspired his literacy efforts as he felt that this comment was the, "first decidedly antislavery lecture" that he heard. Similarly to Tubman, his early life was influenced by religion. He used the New Testament to teach other slaves to read, while more than 40 would attend Sunday school and church services. One such meeting was broken up by plantation owners of the area that were opposed to this activity. They struck with clubs, and threw stones, as they dispersed the group. Also, as with Tubman, this early Biblical teaching continued into adulthood as Douglass joined a black church and affiliated with Christian efforts towards emancipation in the U.S.

Ironically, Douglass did not encounter equality even in his religious pursuits. In the South, he was a member of the Methodist Church. Unfortunately, in an address given at a meeting of the Plymouth County Anti-Slavery Society on November 4, 1841, he related his experience at a Methodist communion service in the North:

> After the good minister had served out the bread and wine to one portion of those near him, he said, "These may withdraw, and others come forward;" thus he proceeded till all the white members had been served. Then he took a long breath, and looking out towards the door, exclaimed, "Come up, colored friends, come up! For you know God is no respecter of persons!" I haven't been there to see the sacraments taken since." [24]

This was not an isolated event, or sentiment, as he further related in the same speech:

> "At New Bedford, where I live, there was a great revival of religion not long ago—many were converted and 'received' as they said, 'into the kingdom of heaven.' But it seems the kingdom of heaven is like a net; at least so it was according to the practice of these pious Christians; and when the net was drawn ashore, they had to set down and cull up the fish. Well, it happened now that some of the fish had rather black scales; so these were sorted out and packed by themselves. But among those who experienced religion at this time was a colored girl; she was baptized in the same water as the rest; so she thought she might sit at the Lord's table and partake of the same sacramental elements with the others. The deacon handed round the cup, and when he came to the black girl, he could not pass her, for there was the minister looking right at him, and as he was a kind of abolitionist, the deacon was rather afraid of giving him offense; so he handed the girl the cup; and she tasted. Now it so happened that next to her sat a young lady who had been converted at the same time, baptized in the same water, and put her trust in the same blessed Savior; yet when the cup containing the precious blood which had been shed for all, came to her, she rose in disdain, and walked out of the church. Such was the religion she experienced!
> Another young lady fell into a trance, when she awoke, she declared she had been to heaven. Her friends were all anxious to know what and whom she had seen there; so she told the whole story. But there was one good old lady whose curiosity went beyond that of all the others—and she inquired of the girl that had the vision, if she saw any black folks in heaven? After some hesitation, the reply was, 'Oh! I didn't go into the kitchen.'
> Thus you see, my hearers, this prejudice goes even into the church of God. And there are those who carry it so far that it is disagreeable to them even to think of going to heaven, if colored people are going there too."[25]

---

[24] The Church and Prejudice, The Life and Writings of Frederick Douglass
[25] Frederick Douglass The Church and Prejudice

Douglass also used his personal experience in the southern Methodist Church, where his master was a class teacher, to stress the incongruity of slavery with Biblical teaching. "But all this prejudice sinks into insignificance in my mind, when compared with enormous iniquity of the system which is its cause—the system that sold my four sisters and my brothers into bondage—and which calls in its priests to defend it even from the Bible! His owner, "would talk most sanctimoniously about the dear Redeemer, who was sent 'to preach deliverance to the captives, and set at liberty them that are bruised'—he could pray at morning, pray at noon, and pray at night; yet he could lash up my poor cousin by his two thumbs, and inflict stripes and blows upon his bare back, till the blood streamed to the ground! All the time quoting scripture, for his authority, and appealing to that passage of the Holy Bible which says, 'He that knoweth his master's will, and doeth it not, shall be beaten with many stripes!' Such was the amount of this good Methodist's piety."[26]

By the water shed era of the 1850s, Douglass viewed the status of Blacks in historical terms, as well as Biblical terms. He drew the conclusion that "Negros" had been recognized as citizens of the country the first time in 1776.[27] For interesting artistic verification of this, note the right hand man in the boat as Washington Crosses the Delaware in the painting by Emanuel Gottlieb Leutze. This artist was interestingly a German American who returned to Germany, supporting the 1848 European Revolution with this inspirational, American based topic. This momentous original oil on canvas was momentous both in size, 378.5 cm by 647.7 cm (149" by 255") and momentous in subject. Completed in 1850, it was damaged by smoke in a fire in the artist studio. Critics have noted that the chief subjects, General George Washington and future fellow president, then Lieutenant, James Monroe, were decreased in focus by this haze while the lesser characters remained in sharper focus. While art students and American tourists served as models in his Germany studio, this original painting never crossed the Delaware River, not even the Atlantic Ocean.[28] It was restored and was purchased by the Kunsthalle Bremen. Unfortunately, the British finally overcame the perceived battle scene by bombing it into destruction via the British Royal Air Force in 1942.[29]

The American version of the famed painting was actually a full sized replica, which was completed in 1851 and put on display in New York in October of that year . Prior to the Civil War, it had also been on display in the United States Capitol Rotunda, where it served as an iconic image for Northerners and Southerners. Not surprisingly, given the historic image of the black subject, in the garb of a New England sailor, the painting was used for fund raising for abolitionists and for the Union. Its final home was also in the North, having been purchased in

---

[26] The Church and Prejudice, Frederick Douglass from The Life and Writings of Frederick Douglass by Philip S. Foner

[27] What the Black Man Wants

[28] Anne Hawkes Hutton, Portrait of Patriotism: Washington Crossing the Delaware. Chilton Book Company, 1975

[29] David Hackett Fischer, Washington's Crossing.

1897 by John Stewart Kennedy and donated to the Metropolitan Museum of Art in New York City.[30]

The additional occasions when Douglass felt "Negros" were accepted as citizens were at the time of the writing of the U.S. Constitution, when blacks had been allowed to vote in 11 of the original 13, and during the War of 1812. He acknowledged that at that time General Andrew Jackson addressed potential black military recruits as "fellow-citizens".[31] With the "Rebellion" he felt opportunity for the "immediate, unconditional, and universal" enfranchisement of the black man, in every State in the Union." [32]

As Frederick Douglass astutely recognized, "when you come to frame a conscription bill, the Negro is a citizen again."[33] Looking back he felt that blacks had "been citizen just three times in the history of this government, and it has always been in time of trouble. In time of trouble we are citizens."[i34] He and many others felt that these "citizens" should have been enlisted to help fight for their freedom years earlier. Unfortunately, he felt that some of the same logic that drove manifest destiny was counter- productive in incorporating African Americans into the military, stating that, "the story of our inferiority is an old dodge."[35] In addition, he noted that "wherever men oppress their fellows, wherever they enslave them, they will endeavor to find the needed apology for such enslavement and oppression in the character of the people oppressed and enslaved. When we wanted, a few years ago, a slice of Mexico, it was hinted that the Mexicans were an inferior race, that the old Castilian blood had become so weak that it would scarcely run down- hill, and that Mexico needed the long, strong and beneficent arm of the Anglo-Saxon care extended over it. We said that it was necessary to its salvation, and a part of the 'manifest destiny' of this Republic, to extend our arm over that dilapidated government."[36]

---

[30] David Hackett Fischer, Washington's Crossing. Oxford University Press, 2004

[31] What the Black Man Wants

[32] What the Black Man Wants

[33] What the Black Man Wants

[34] What the Black Man Wants

[35] What the Black Man Wants

[36] The Life and Writings of Frederick Douglass by Philip S. Foner speech What the Black Man Wants

Figure 18 - President Abraham Lincoln

Harper's pg .47, Chapter 7, Manifest Destiny in Slavery

If the Northern culture would have acknowledged the abilities of the black man to serve actively in "manifest destiny" earlier, the Civil War would in all likelihood have ended many months sooner. Unfortunately, Northern white sentiment also needed to change in order to incorporate sizable numbers of African Americans into the Union military. Ironically, while the armies, both Union and Confederate literally cried out for more men, a vast labor pool was considered of minimal value. If either side had efficiently utilized the Black labor pool for the war effort, the War would have taken a much different path..

The actual manpower was and is impossible to know for sure. While the census of 1860 would appear to be the most relevant with which to examine the population demographics of the Southern and Northern areas, this is far from perfect. With the census designed to reflect the United States as of June 1, 1860, this decennial counting was unfortunately greatly affected by the looming War. Unlike any other census efforts, this was the only one that, in a sense, was the counting of two separate, national entities, with the Southern states vying for national recognition. As was documented in a preface to the accounting:

> The volume now presented to Congress includes the returns of population, classified in a manner to illustrate its various relations and afford easy comparison with the past. Every effort has been made to insure accuracy, and, it is believed, with success. While errors may occur, it is confidently believed that they will be of minor importance, and less in number than have appeared in any previous census. It has been the aim of the Superintendent to make the work of value to the people, by combining with the figures some general information on the subjects of which they treat; and in attempting this he has adhere closely to truth, and hazarded no statements unwarranted by the figures. It is not impossible, in view of the contrariety of belief existing among a reflecting people, that we have made deductions distasteful to some, and at variance with the preconceived opinions of others; but as the mission of statistics is to develop the truth, we have endeavored to exhibit their teachings fairly, fully, and impartially, although in so doing we have been compelled, at times, to represent results differently from what we would have wished the facts to warrant.[37]

Ultimately, this census was completed with difficulties and truly reflects "results differently from what we would have wished the facts to warrant."[38] Despite discrepancies in records, the mere survival of these records from this tumultuous upheaval that followed is remarkable.

> Fortunately for the interests of statistics, the unhappy insurrection which developed itself so soon after the eighth decennial enumeration was completed, was not the occasion of the detention or loss of any of the returns, and we are enabled to present a true statement of the condition of the population immediately preceding the lamentable civil war which has impeded immigration, occasioned the interruption of much of our foreign commerce and internal trade, and been attended with more desolation than will ever be developed by the pen of history or realized by posterity, because of the recuperative energies of our people, the accelerated flow of migration, and the natural fertility and reintegrating (sic) nature of our lands. The rebellion, however, has not been without its effect upon satisfactory progress in the compilation of the census, in that it

---

[37] Census of the United States 1860

[38] Census of the United States 1860

has interrupted communication with many of the marshals, and to some small extent with the South, precluded the possibility of that interchange of correspondence necessary to insure completeness in the arrangement of some of the minor details. The same cause has naturally led to clerical changes and induced a condition of excitement and restlessness unfavorable to the rapid compilation of a work demanding for its proper execution a good degree of experience and the most patient application.[39]

Despite this assurance of the accuracy of the report, this census was abbreviated compared to the expected decennial epochs. Particularly lacking were cartographic representations of the data. Fortunately, though, the statistics did lead to the generation of maps of use to Union commanders. Furthermore, this was only the second census to include every member of each household, in its enumeration. This included women, children and slaves. Prior to the 1850 census, only the head of household and overall total number of household members were specified. By the 1860 tallying, the statistics were designed to be the most detailed ever carried out in the United States.

An example, of this increasing meticulous enumeration, was the inclusion in the June 1860 count of "Native Americans." This count was, ironically, only inclusive of those of American Indian descent who had "renounced tribal rules." These were listed at 40,000 individuals.[40]

Despite these idiosyncrasies, the research did lead to useful reports. Especially helpful were general numbers of white residents, ages of prospective troops, slaves, and agricultural products by county. Railroad and post-road routes were formulated into useful maps and terrain was defined in terms of cultivation of arable land. This information was particularly useful to armies that would advance, living off the land, without traditional supply train support. The areas, by county level detail, were further defined in terms of commerce and manufacturing.

Also, included were interesting observations of the means of subsistence and references to the number of persons sustainable by the cultivation of the land. It was felt that census numbers in 1860 already reflected, "an excess of inhabitants beyond what the ordinary cultivation of the soil can sustain."[41] Significantly, this limit was thought to have been reached in the "New England States—Massachusetts, Rhode Island, and Connecticut—which contain 13,780 square miles." The actual total population of these three states increased by over 350,000, from 1,512,851 to 1,865,833, and the number of inhabitants to the square mile within these states averaged about 107 in 1850 and approximately 130 in 1860.[42] The gist of the logic stated that, "the cultivated area of these States has increased comparatively little in fifty years; nevertheless they go on increasing in population with a rapidity as great as at any former period of their history."[43]

---

[39] Census of the US 1860

[40] Census of the US 1860

[41] Census of 1860

[42] Census of 1860

[43] Census of 1860, Introduction

While Northern leaders could view these numbers with ambivalence, Southern leaders had far less consolation in population numbers or in rate of growth. It was also considered significant that in 1860 South Carolina, "It is, perhaps, a little remarkable that the relative increase of the free colored class in this State was more considerable than that of any other. As their number, 9,914, is so small as to excite neither apprehension nor jealousy among the white race, the increase is probably due both to manumission and natural causes. This State has made slower progress during the last term than any other in the South, having advanced only from 27.28 to 28.72 inhabitants to the square mile." Surprisingly, even Virginia had only a 12.29 per cent increase in total population between 1850 and 1860. Also, significantly for the prospect of victory in civil war, the white population increased 17.06 per cent in these ten years, while slaves increased 3.88 per cent in this state.

Not boding well for the chance of victory, based on basic population totals, the three slowest growing states were South Carolina, Tennessee, and Virginia. The states with the most rapid increase in population were New York and Pennsylvania. These bastions of the Union demonstrated nearly incredible growth in this one decade. New York state alone increased by over ¾ of a million, or 25.29%, in large part due to immigration. Very interestingly, in New York state in 1860, the "free colored population has fallen off 64 since 1850, a diminution to be accounted for, probably, by the operation of the fugitive slave law, which induced many colored persons to migrate further north." Some likely relocated to Pennsylvania, where the "free colored" population increased approximately by 3,000 over the same decade. In the estimation of census analysts, this migration reflected, "The greater mildness of the climate" (really?) "and a milder type of the prejudices connected with this class of population, the result of benevolent influences and its proximity to the slaveholding States."

Another Northern state that was exemplary in growth, and that furthers the argument that the South stood a better chance of victory in rebellion in 1850 rather than in 1860, was Illinois. Its 101% gain in ten years was felt to be "the most wonderful example of great, continuous, and healthful increase." Despite the tingeing of this image by some former Governors and Al Capone a century later, this "condition to which Illinois has attained under the progress of the last thirty years is a monument of the blessings of industry, enterprise, peace, and free institutions." Even Indiana, likewise, had "most satisfactory" growth in population. While Michigan, Wisconsin and Iowa were felt to have "participated to the full extent in the surprising development of the Northwest," this was reasoned to be related to "The remarkable healthfulness of the climate of that region seems to more than compensate for its rigors, and the fertility of the new soil leads men eagerly to contend with and overcome the harshness of the elements." The fruit of these labors was to place these "States of the Northwest" to become the "granary of Europe, and that section of our Union which, within the recollection of living men, was a wilderness, is now the chief source of supply in seasons of scarcity for the suffering millions of another continent." These resources did not relieve suffering as picturesquely during the civil strife, as both both Northern and Southern prisoner-of-war accounts attest.

Chapter Seven - Natural Selection, Survival of the Fittest

By 1860, the United States was comprised of nineteen states without legal slavery, seven territories, and fifteen slaveholding states and the unique District of Columbia. In the most general terms, the total population in slave states increased 27.33 per cent between 1850 and 1860. The free states, District of Columbia, and seven Territories increased 41.24 percent in total population. The actual numbers increased 2,627,000 in total in the slave states and 19,203,008 in the free areas. On the most pragmatic level, if Civil War had been initiated basically one decade earlier, the stilted population numbers would have been less stilted. This was explained, "It is due to candor to state that the marked disproportion between the rate of gain in the north and south, respectively, is manifestly to some extent caused by the larger number of immigrants who settle in the former section, on account of congeniality of climate, the variety of occupation, the dignity wherewith respectable employment is invested, and the freedom of labor."[44] This same logic could have been repeated in the twentieth and twenty first centuries to ironically justify some aspects of the growth in the population of the Sun Belt.

The financial investment in human chattel also increased incredibly during this same decade. By 1860, the slave population had increased 23.44 percent, thereby magnifying the potential economic impact of a Civil War loss for the South in 1860 versus 1850. In an interesting microcosm of mid-nineteen century society, though, the District of Columbia actually had a decrease of 502 slaves between the 1850 and 1860 census. In the documentation of this fact in the Census Report of June 1, 1860, an interesting prescience would appear to be in effect. "By a law of April 16, 1862, slavery has been abolished in the District of Columbia, the owners of slaves having been compensated out of the public treasury." This aberrancy is related to the impact of Civil War, with the more complete version of the 1860 census published in 1864.[45] (see table on pg 600 reflecting entire population class growth 1790-1860.)

Despite claims, "the unhappy insurrection which developed itself so soon after the eighth decennial enumeration was completed, was not the occasion of the detention or loss of any of the returns, and we are enabled to present a true statement of the condition of the population immediately preceding the lamentable civil war which has impeded immigration, occasioned the interruption of much of our foreign commerce and internal trade, and been attended with more desolation than will ever be developed by the pen of history or realized by posterity, because of the recuperative energies of our people, the accelerated flow of migration, and the natural fertility and redintegrating (sic) nature of our lands. The rebellion, however, has not been without its effect upon satisfactory progress in the compilation of the census, in that it has

---

[44] Census of 1860 page vii

[45] Census of 1860 Introduction, pg vii

interrupted communication with many of the marshals, and to some small extent with the South, precluded the possibility of that interchange of correspondence necessary to insure completeness in the arrangement of some of the minor details."[46]

It is, of course, impossible to ascertain the accuracy of this reassurance. What true "minor details" were adulterated, omitted, or falsified in the interest of national security can never be known with certainty. It was admitted that the pending hostilities, "naturally led to clerical changes, and induced a condition of excitement and restlessness (REALLY!?) unfavorable to the rapid compilation of a work demanding for its proper execution a good degree of experience and the most patient application."

Interestingly, a substantial amount of employee discontentment was voiced in this unexpected format. It was less than eloquently stated, "To render the census as useful and available as the materials admit, our people must realize what the experience and practice of other governments teach---that the proper development of a nation's standing and progress demands the agency of a permanent foundation, offering encouragement to capacity and fidelity by insuring continuous and remunerative employment to such as prove their qualifications for usefulness." [47]

It is useful to note that this qualification for US Government employment was not documented by mandatory Civil Service examinations until 1883. The Pendleton Civil Service Reform Act, enacting this testing, was a direct result of the assassination of President James Garfield by a, "disgruntled office seeker." Replacing the traditional political spoils system, employment was to be based on merit and actual skills.

---

[46] US census Introduction

[47] US census Introduction

INDIAN SQUAWS WINNOWING WHEAT.

Figure 19 - American Indians-repressed and under-appreciated. Harper's pg. 283

Figure 20 - Delaware Indians Acting as Scouts in the West for the Union. Leslie's pg. 257

The 1860 census, the 8th of the United States, was overseen by Joseph Camp Griffith Kennedy, a product of this spoils system. Entitled the, " Superintendent of Census," Kennedy acted as supervisor for both the 1850 and 1860 censuses. This plum position was awarded to this multifaceted man in reward for political activism in a 1848 election in his home state of Pennsylvania. Kennedy was a son of a distinguished farming family and very well educated for his time, having graduated from Allegheny College, in Meadville, Pennsylvania with MA degree in 1856 and LLD, law degree, in 1864. He was fundamentally a Whig, lawyer and journalist. Serving as census supervisor to the Under Secretary of the Interior, he helped redesign forms, carried out communication with Congress and sought to improve the usefulness of the decennial accounting. Very unfortunately, Mr. Kennedy was dropped from the US census when he was tragically stabbed to death on July 13, of 1887 by a disgruntled business associate named John Daily.

In his department of 1860, 184 clerks labored to produce the abbreviated report. This information had been largely gathered on the most local level by marshals. On the upper end of the census system, overseeing Kennedy and hundreds of other workers, was the Secretary of the Interior. From 3/10/1857 to 1/8/1861 this position was held by Jacob Thompson. As only the 5th US Secretary of the Interior, Thompson was a son of the South and soon revealed his loyalty to the Confederacy. Born in Leasburg, North Carolina on May 15, 1810, Mr. Thompson was, like the future Under Secretary, well-educated for his time. Graduating from the University of North Carolina in 1831, he likewise studied law and began legal practice in Pontotoc, Mississippi in 1834.[48] By five years later, he was elected to the 26th United States Congress and served his adopted state from 1839 to 1851. During this tenure, he also served as chairman of the Committee on Indian Affairs. In 1857 he resumed his law practice after losing a reelection bid. This return to private practice was short lived as Thompson accepted an appointment to President James Buchanan's cabinet, as Secretary to the Interior, in the same year.[49]

With little in the way of competition, Secretary Thompson stands out as a most remarkable public servant. As a true Southerner, his loyalty to the Union came to a breaking point in early 1861. On January 8 of this year, this cabinet member resigned to join the Confederacy and was soon serving as Inspector General of the Confederate States Army. Although not trained formally in the military, Thompson followed a common path into Confederate army service and advanced to the rank of Lt. Colonel. While in the Confederacy, he undoubtedly had

---

[48] Biographical Directory of the United States Congress

[49] Bio dir of US congress

opportunity to employ his knowledge gained from the supervision of the U.S. census. No lesser a paper than the New York Daily Tribune actually listed him "a traitor." Stating in the stirring rhetoric of the volatile period of secession, "Undertaking to overthrow the Government of which you are a sworn minister may be in accordance with the ideas of cotton-growing chivalry, but to common men cannot be made to appear creditable."[50]

Remarkably, Thompson appeared capable outside of the usual duties of "a traitor" by serving as an aide to Confederate General P.T. Beauregard and participated in various military actions including Shiloh, Vicksburg, Tupelo and Corinth. By March of 1864, the Confederate President, Jefferson Davis, had taken note of Thompson's talents and requested that he oversee a Confederate secret mission into Canada. While in Montreal he supervised unsuccessful actions in the Great Lakes, including an attempt to rescue Confederate prisoners of war on Johnson's Island in Lake Erie. Probably his most notorious and inflammatory action, whether or not he was actually involved, centered on plotting to set a fire in New York City on November 25, 1864. Ironically, the Union did successfully burn down his home, "Home Place", in Oxford, Mississippi also in this same year. As the ultimate traitor action, though, Thompson headed Confederate spies and was rumored to have had contact with John Wilkes Booth and may have had some role in the assassination or kidnapping attempt of President Abraham Lincoln. The former Secretary of the Interior under Lincoln's predecessor denied this. Due to these allegations, Thompson went abroad, first to England and then to Canada, before returning to the reunited south, settling in Memphis, Tennessee. He continued to be financially successful in his personal affairs and served on the board at the University of the South at Sewanee before passing away in 1885.[51]

After the resignation of Confederate Jacob Thompson, the further census work of the Union was under the jurisdiction of the 6th Secretary of the Interior, Caleb Blood Smith.[52] As a product of the political spoils system, this Secretary was also noteworthy. Although born in Boston, Massachusetts in 1808, a year before his future boss, Abraham Lincoln, he moved to Ohio in 1814. Similarly to Thompson, Smith became a lawyer, serving in the Indiana legislature and then in the United States Congress in 1843-1849. Also similarly he returned to private law practice in Cincinnati, Ohio and in Indianapolis, Indiana. By 1860, this Whig played a significant role in the Republican National Convention held in Chicago. By assisting in nominating Lincoln for the Republican candidacy for the president, he earned appointment to Lincoln's cabinet as Secretary of the Interior in 1861.

Ironically, this Secretary, similarly to Thompson, left the position after conflict related to the Civil War. He resigned in December 1862 with poor health and with disappointment with the Lincoln administration over the policy to slaves as documented in the Emancipation

---

[50] New York Daily Tribune, January 9, 1861, page 4

[51] Jacob Thompson Collection, in William and Marjorie Lewis Collection at the University of Mississippi in Archives and Special Collections

[52] Biographical Directory of the United States Congress

Proclamation.[53] He died at the age of 55, on January 7, 1864. He was succeeded as Secretary of the Interior by the experienced Under Secretary of the Interior, John Palmer Usher. Usher was credited with much of the work on the census of 1860, and on the more unabridged version of 1864.

---

[53] Biographical Directory of the United States Congress

Chapter Nine - A Decree Was Issued that a Census Should Take Place

The turnover in the Interior Department was addressed in the 1860 Census Introduction, "The nature of this office, at present, holds out no such incentives; but, on the contrary, its most valued employees are induced to seek positions in other bureaus, which give higher remuneration and promise more permanent employment."[54] Apparently, Secretary Thompson's move to the Government of the Confederacy was an example of this employment trend.

The actual data collection was the burden of the U.S. Marshals, their assistants and if necessary military personnel. The specific instructions for 1860 were generally thought to follow those of 1850. In the History and Growth of the United States Census (1790-1890) by Wright and Hunt, page 51, it was stated that only minor changes had occurred between the two immediately antebellum enumerations. However, in a public record from Frederick G. Bohme, Chief, History Branch, Data User Services Division, dated December 23, 1993, he documents that Judy Austin, at the Library of Congress, recently located a "single copy of the 1860 instructions."[55]

Of greatest significance, instructions of 1860 specified, "who taxed Indians are and how they are to be enumerated—by writing "Ind." under the color (race) heading. (On the schedule, that column provides only for "White, black (note that use of this term began in 1850), and mulatto."

Also, "The 1860 manuscript schedules for California, which led to exact tabulations of "Asiatics," (sic) show that the enumerators also entered "Chinese" or "Mongolian" in the color column in 1860."[56] Interestingly, "to see the further development of census confidentiality from 1850-1860: People can see the population schedules, but now only for the purpose of correcting errors, and the enumerator now may tell respondents, if necessary, that access to the "products of industry" schedule is restricted."[57]

This Census Law was fundamentally, "An Act providing for the taking of the Seventh and subsequent Censuses of the United States, and to fix the number of the members of the House

---

[54] Introduction to the 1860 Census

[55] United States Department of Commerce, Bureau of the Census, memorandum For the Record, December 23,1993

[56] Boehm memorandum

[57] Boehm Memorandum

of Representatives, and provide for their future apportionment among the several States."[58] This document also states the "Duties, Liabilities, and Compensation of Marshals" in a legalistic run on sentence: "Be it enacted by the Senate and House of Representatives of the United States of America in Congress assembled, That the marshals of the several districts of the United States, including the District of Columbia and the Territories, are hereby required respectively to cause all the inhabitants to be enumerated, and to collect all the other statistical information within their respective districts, in the manner provided for in this act, and specified in the instructions which shall be given by the Secretary of the Interior, and in the tables annexed, and to return the same to the said Secretary of or before the first day of November next ensuing, omitting from the enumeration of the inhabitants Indians not taxed; also, at the discretion of said Secretary, any part or all the statistics of the Territories, except those of population: Provided, however, And if the time assigned for making the returns shall prove inadequate for the Territories, the said Secretary may extend the same: Provided, further, If there be any District or Territory of the United States in which there is no marshal of the United States, the President shall appoint some suitable person to discharge the duties assigned by this act to marshals."[59]

Each Marshall was responsible to define districts of his district. These subdivisions were to be based upon defined borders, such as "known civil divisions, such as county, parish, township, town, ward, or district lines, or highways, or natural boundaries, such as rivers, lakes, &c."[60] Assistants were to be appointed. They were to be residents of the area that were assigned to enumerate, authorized by commissions, and supplied with written instructions from the Department of the Interior, in addition to the actual census blank forms. Two copies of each form were to be filed. After review by the Marshal, one copy was to be forwarded to the Secretary of the Interior and the other transmitted to the "office of the secretary of the State or Territory to which his district belongs."[61]

In separating his district into manageable areas for the door to door work, instructions mandated that these were not to exceed twenty thousand persons in each. (How did he do this without the census?) If this "number causes inconvenient boundaries, in which case the number may be larger."[62] Simultaneously, the Marshals were to report, from most reliable sources available to him, the estimated square miles contained in his defined areas. This estimation of area covered was very important, as it figured into the calculation of financial compensation for the assistants. In return for the actual act of gathering information, "the service required of him by a personal visit to each dwelling-house, and to each family, in the subdivision assigned to him, and shall ascertain, by inquiries made of some member of each

---

[58] Eight Census, United States-1860

[59] 8th Census

[60] Instructions to U.S. Marshals 1860 Census, Sec. 3

[61] Instructions to U.S. Marshals 1860 Census, Sec. 5

[62] Census Law sec. 3

family, if any one can be found capable of giving the information, but if not, then of the agent of such family, the name of each member thereof, the age and place of birth of each, and all the other particulars specified in this act, the tables thereto subjoined, and the instructions of the Secretary of the Interior; and shall also visit personally the farms, mills, shops, mines, and other places respecting which information in required as above specified, in his district, and shall obtain all such information from the best and most reliable sources; and when in either case the information is obtained and entered on the tables, as obtained, till the same is complete, then such memoranda shall be immediately read to the person or persons furnishing the facts, to correct errors and supply omissions if any shall exist."[63]

Within one month of the designated date of completion of his count, his signature was to be affixed to each page, listing on the last page the number of pages in the specific return, and original forms returned to the clerk of the assigned county. Additionally, two copies were to be returned to the Marshal, one of which was to be forwarded to the Secretary of the Interior and the other to the secretary of the Territory or State which had been enumerated.[64] As remuneration for these efforts, each assistant was to be paid two cents for each individual enumerated. An additional ten cents per mile was allotted for travel expenses. A remarkable formula was used to calculate the numbers of miles travelled in the line of taking the census. Cumbersomely, this was "to be ascertained by multiplying the square root of the number of dwelling-houses in the division by the square root of the number of square miles in each division, and the product shall be taken as the number of miles travelled, for all purposes."[65]

Fortunately, additional pay was allocated, beyond the price per individual counted, at the rate of ten cents for each farm return and fifteen cents per return from a "productive industry."[66]

In another eloquent statement, "for the social statistics, two per cent, upon the amount allowed for the enumeration of population, and for each name of a deceased person returned, two cents."[67] From whom this information was attained is unrecorded. Forfeiture of wages and penalties were also well defined for any assistant or Marshal who did not follow the letter of the law. This was from five hundred to five thousand dollars and imprisonment of not less than two years, based on the level of infraction.

The actual cost of the return of the forms was to be paid to the Post Office Department, with twelve thousand dollars set aside from the U.S. Treasury for the returns, themselves, and other documents directly related to the Census. By a franking technique, the cover was to be written on with "official business, census" and further endorsed with the name of the assistant

---

[63] Eight Census Sec. 10

[64] Eight Census Sec. 11

[65] Section 12

[66] Sect 13

[67] Sect 13

or marshal that generated the packet.[68] By Act Supplementary to the Law of May 23, 1850, it was further enacted that compensation was increased for the assistants and marshals taking the Seventh Census in the wide spread areas of California, New Mexico, Utah, and Oregon.[69]

The rate to complete and return the forms was increased to eight cents per page for the original two copies, as specified under the eleventh section of the prior act, of which this was a supplement.[70]

Compensation for the officers of this census effort was significant. As opposed to the piece work of underlings, the superintending clerk in the census office was salaried at the rate of two thousand five hundred dollars per annum. His immediate assistants and clerks were to be paid at a going rate for such office work as defined by the Secretary of the Interior. No salary for these workers was to exceed one thousand dollars per year.[71] There was some hope of wages for the Secretary of the Census Board beyond the above stated $3000.00. "Out of any money in the treasury not otherwise appropriated, one hundred and fifty thousand dollars, may be allowed to this Secretary by the Secretary of the Interior."[72]

---

[68] Sect. 17

[69] Census Law Act Supplementary to the Law of May 23, 1850, pg 6, section 1 of Instructions to U.S. Marshals

[70] Census Law Act Supplementary to the Law of May 23, 1850, p 6, section 3

[71] Instructions to U.S. Marshals, section 19

[72] Section 20

Chapter Ten - The 8th Census, That Took Place While Usher Was Undersecretary

The most direct impact on the impending hostilities, to be defined by this Census, was the apportionment of representation in the U.S. House of Representatives. This responsibility, with its profound political impact, was the duty of the Secretary of the Interior. In additional legal eloquence, "it shall be the duty of the Secretary of the Interior to ascertain the aggregate representative population of the United States, by adding to the whole number of free persons in all the States, including those bound to service for a term of years, and excluding Indians not taxed, three-fifths of all other persons; which aggregate population he shall divide by the number two hundred and thirty-three, and the product of such division, reflecting any fraction of an unit, if any such happen to remain, shall be the ratio or rule of apportionment of representatives among the several States under such enumeration; and the said Secretary of the Department of the Interior shall then proceed, in the same manner, to ascertain the representative population of each State, and to divide the whole number of the representative population (sic) of each State, and to divide the whole number of the representative population of each State by the ratio already determined by him, as above directed; and the product of this last division shall be the number of representatives apportioned to such State under the then last enumeration: *Provided,* That the loss in the number of members caused by the fractions remaining in the several States, on the division of the population thereof, shall be compensated for by assigning to so many States having the largest fractions one additional member each for its fraction, as may be necessary to make the whole number of representatives two hundred and thirty-three: *And provided, also,* That if, after the apportionment of the representatives under the next or any subsequent census, a new State or States shall be admitted in the Union, the representative or representatives assigned to such new State or States shall be in addition to the number of representatives herein above limited; which excess of representatives over two hundred and thirty-three shall only continue until the next succeeding apportionment of representatives under the next succeeding census."[73]

Responsibility for accuracy and completeness was emphasized directly to the assistants and to the Marshals, themselves. In the language of the time, "*Finally.*—The duty entrusted for your execution" (Yikes, what a penalty! Followed by more descriptive wording.) "is one of the most important which could be conferred, as upon the result of your labors must depend the establishment of the ratio of representation, and the just and equitable apportionment of members of the House of Representatives, a fair exhibition of the material resources of the country, and true return of the moral and social condition of each State and Territory. That you will execute this trust with fidelity and zeal, is the expectation and hope of the head of the

---

[73] Section 25

department, by whose orders, in conformity with law, these instructions are issued."[74] Apparently, the position carried the potential of abuse and personal gain beyond aforementioned legitimate pay. Documented misuse of confidential information had been an issue, in prior censuses and reinforcement of federal policy and penalties for infractions were included in the correspondence that each assistant was to keep with himself consistently on his appointed rounds. The General Instructions in Taking The Eighth Census addresses, under the "*Address*" section, mentions the specific indiscretion of "one or two indiscreet assistants engaged in taking the Seventh Census, by the liberty exercised in the unnecessary exposure of facts relating to the business and pursuits of individuals, the communication of intelligence obtained in the discharge of duty to persons who desired it for private advantage or pecuniary profit, or to newspapers."[75]

Access to informants was obviously the basis for all this governmentally mandated questioning. By law, the assistants were to be residents of their assigned districts and were to be familiar with fellow citizens and businesses. After being duly sworn in and commissioned, necessary forms, called "schedules, and a suitable portfolio for their preservation, wherein they should be carried without folding." The most logical and durable portfolio would have been leather, appropriately stiff, and oiled to assist in water protection. Assistants, themselves, were to supply their own portable inkstand or inkwell, a suitable supply of ink, and pens. These were, of course of dip pen style and each portfolio was to be "accompanied with a sheet of blotting paper with which you will carefully dry all entries made on the schedules."[76]

Six schedules were present and were to have individual sheets numbered sequentially, in the order of their completion. Needless to say, handwriting had to be legible and non-smudged.

Every two weeks, each assistant in the field was to advise his supervising Marshal of his progress, without delay. Marshals were expected to follow up on any delays. "Dilatoriness, therefore, on the part of any Assistant should meet with immediate reprehension. Unnecessary procrastination, or any other cause (which might by timely caution be avoided) tending to defeat the proper consummation of duty, involves the abatement of compensation and liability to penalty—a contingency which it is hoped will never occur."[77] Financial remuneration was timed to reinforce timely returns with one half of earned pay to be paid only after schedules were delivered and reviewed for completeness and clarity. For perpetual reinforcement of these guidelines, "*At all times have this pamphlet of Instructions with you.*"[78]

Cooperation, particularly with increasing hostilities between North and South, was hoped to be obtained on each doorstep through charm, appropriate manners, and, if necessary, through threats. If a person refused to answer questions or intentionally misrepresented their

---

[74] Pg. 10 of Instructions to Marshals

[75] Pg. 12

[76] General Instructions in Taking the Eighth Census, item #2

[77] Instruction to Marshals, item 15, page 10

[78] General Instructions in Taking the Eighth Census, item #4

information, the Assistant was to "inform him of the responsibility he incurs thereby, and the penalty to which he becomes liable under the 15th section of the law."[79] Discretion regarding which schedule was to be used and, therefore, what questions were to be included in each interview was up to the Marshal. This fact alone was a possible point of contention. The most obvious variation in questioning was over Schedule 2, relating to the slave population, which was to be omitted in free States.

The race of the individual being enumerated would have been addressed initially on the census form under the "Special Instructions" of Schedule No. 1—Free Inhabitants.[80] "*Color*— Under heading 6, entitled '*Color*,' in all cases where the person is white leave the space blank; in all cases where the person is black, without admixture insert the letter 'B;' if a mulatto, or of mixed blood, write 'M;' if an Indian, write 'Ind.' It is very desirable to have these directions carefully observed."[81] Schedule No. 2—"SLAVE INHABITANTS", was used for the final time in this accounting of 1860. Emphasis was placed on defining, "Owners of Slaves," and "the desire is to obtain a true return of the number of owners."[82] It was stressed that slaves held in ownership by more than one individual do not appear as "owners in other places."[83] After this recording of the owner name, the number of slaves owned was to be listed. As further attestation of the dehumanization of slavery, numbers were to be used in place of names for the slaves, themselves. Each individual slave of a given owner was to be numbered separately and sequentially in order of age, with the oldest listed as Number 1. If these slaves were rented out, employed by a person, plantation, or business other than by the documented owner, the owner was to be listed as the "proprietor" while the entity or person employing them was to be noted as "employer."[84]

As instructed for tallying the white population, the age of children less than one year of age as of the 1st day of June, 1860, was to be recorded as a fractional part of the year. Likewise to the white population, slaves were to be listed as living even if they had died prior to this 1st day of June, upon which the Census field work formally started. Very noteworthy and another example of eloquence and clarity was the fact that, "Slaves who (born previously) have died since the 1st day of June are to be entered as living, and all details respecting them to be given with as much care as if the slave were living. You are desired to give the names of all slaves whose age reaches or exceeds 100 years."[85] Despite this instruction to list the "names," of these slaves, the *Sex* column, under heading number 4, instructions specifically stressed the

---

[79] General Instructions in Taking the Eighth Census #6.

[80] Schedule No. 1, pg 15, point 9. Color

[81] Section 9. Page 15, Special Instructions, Schedule No. 1 Census 1860

[82] Schedule No. 2, page 17, point 1.

[83] same

[84] Page 18, No. 2

[85] Pg 18 point 3

importance of indicating "m" for male and "f" for female due to the "entire omission of name."[86]

To ascertain that this order would be carried out, financial compensation to the census taker was to be reduced if this gender was not specified.[87]

"Color" was to be recorded as on returns or schedules for the "free" population. Also, any slaves that "absconded" or escaped, and had not been returned to the owner, within the prior year were to be recorded as if in possession of the owner. This specific blank was to be filled in with either a number or mark, opposite of the name of the legal owner. Slaves that had been most fortunate and manumitted within the year prior to the date of July 1, 1860, were to be indicated as such in column No. 7. In contrast, those slaves who were probably the least fortunate, were enumerated in column No. 8. This space was to indicated the number and general description of slaves who were, *"Deaf and Dumb, Blind, Insane, Idiotic"* and was also used to enumerate any slaves that were imprisoned convicts, with the crime to be listed here.

In the delineation of "deaf," it was to be further designated if the individual was born deaf, or if became deaf prior to acquiring speech skills. Likewise, census takers were encouraged to specify if blindness was from a certain definable cause. Fascinatingly, the definition of an individual as *"Insane"* or *"Idiotic"* was not believed to be as straight forward as deafness and blindness. In the language of the mid-nineteenth century, and prior to patient confidentiality issues, "The various degrees of insanity often create a doubt as to the propriety of thus classifying individuals, and demands (sic) the exercise of discretion. A person may be reputed erratic on some subject, but if competent to manage his or her business affairs without manifesting any symptoms of insanity to an ordinary observer, such person should not be recorded as insane. Seemingly, as a fellow member of the same community as the enumerated, the census taker would have possibly attained this "ordinary observer" status on more than this census driven visit. Comfortingly, the insanity diagnosis would be much easier for this lay person to detect, if the enumerated were, "in institutions for safety or restoration." If residing in such a place, "there can exist no doubt as to how you should classify them." Additionally of interest was the "general rule, the term Insanity applies to individuals who have once possessed mental faculties which have become impaired; whereas *Idiocy* applies to persons who have never possessed vigorous mental faculties, but from their birth have manifested aberration. The cases wherein it may be difficult to distinguish between insanity and idiocy are not numerous; should such occur, however, you may rely on the opinion of any physician to whom the case is known."[88]

As in the specification of deafness, underlying pathology was to be ferreted out and included on the schedule. "In all cases of insane persons, you will write in the space where you enter the word "Insane," the *cause* of such insanity; and you will in every case inquire into the cause or origin thereof, and write the word—as intemperance, spiritualism, grief, affliction, hereditary,

---

[86]Pg. 18 point 4

[87]Pg 18 point 4

[88]Pg 16, point 18

misfortune, &c. As nearly every case of insanity may be traced to some known cause, it is earnestly desired that you will not fail to make your return in this respect as perfect as possible."[89]

Similarly, in an antebellum, now socially unacceptable association, the mental health issues were further grouped with *Paupers* and *Convicts.* "If any person whose name you record be at the time, or within the year, so indigent or destitute of the means of support as to require the support of the community, obtained either by alms-begging or public maintenance, by taxation or poor fund, you are to write the word 'pauper' in column 14, on a line with the name of such person." [90] Also, in this same column, it was noted that, "When persons who have been convicted of crime within the year resided, on the 1st of June, in any family you enumerate, the fact should be stated by fiving in column 14, on a line with the name, the character of the crime; but as such an interrogatory might five offence you had better, where you can do so, refer to the county records for the information, but use care in applying the crime to the proper individual on the schedule." Unlike the situation where the census taker was assigned the duty of making and disclosing psychiatric diagnosis of a neighbor, more care was to be taken in the release of criminal information. "With the county or parish record, and your own knowledge, you will be able to make this return very correctly without occasioning offence by personal inquiry of individuals."[91]

Similarly, more emphasis was placed on confidentiality issues in business schedules than in mental health disclosures. It was anticipated that more resistance was to be encountered from business owners than from other classes of the population. In this instance, the Assistant Marshal, seeking this information, was to reassure anonymity, and that "The primary facts are confidentially received and will only be published in connexion (sic) with, and as a part of, a great body of similar facts, from which it will be impossible to abstract or distinguish those of individual firms or corporations. Individual statements are necessary for the formation of aggregate results. If necessary you may state that examination of the returns is not permitted for any private purpose, nor does the Department allow access to them for other than public uses."[92]

Of even more value to the soon to be combatants, North and South, were the definition of resources, industry and products of each region. Agriculture, the returns of all farms or plantations, was delineated in Schedule No. 4. Only agricultural plots and lots, "owned or worked by persons following mechanical or other pursuits, or where the productions are not one hundred dollars in value," were to be omitted. The quantity of improved land reflected the actual number of acres which had been cleared and under use during the year ending on the 1st of June, 1860. This included acreage, meadows, arable land, and pasture which had been "reclaimed from a state of nature, and which continues to be reclaimed and used for the

---

[89]Pg 17

[90]Pg 17

[91]Pg 17, point 18

[92]Pg. 24, Schedule No. 5

purposes of production."[93] In contrast, the number of acres of "Unimproved Land," was simplistically as land owned by each proprietor that did not meet the definition of "Improved Land."

An example would be a wood or timber lot which is used for the farm. Interestingly, swamps, marshes or bogs, viewed as "unimprovable," (sic) were not to be enumerated or included. Lakes or ponds covering more than 10 acres, likewise, were not to be included.[94] In stark contrast to evaluation in the next century, these water features were not environmentally viewed as an asset.

Through much of the following questioning of the farmer or plantation owner, the monetary value of the farm was to be listed, carefully and particularly in round figures. Furthermore, equipment or implements used on the farm were to be evaluated as an aggregate. Examples, again of specific use to warring factions, included cotton gins, wagons, sugar-mills, and threshing machinery. The products of such agricultural pursuits were to be defined separately.

Amount and value of produce was to be identified in appropriate units of quantity, such as pounds, bushels, bales, tons, etc. A very popular produce of the time, molasses, was to be defined as coming from "M" for maple or "S" for sorgum (sic), and leaving space blank for column 44 if the molasses is from cane source.[95]

Similarly of potentially benefit to advancing armies, at times foraging for necessary resources without supply train support, was information listed on "Schedule No. 5—Products of Industry."[96] Reassurance would have been given that "Should any one object on the ground of *not wishing to expose the nature of his business,* the Assistant Marshal should state that it is not desired to elicit any information which shall be used or published in connexion (sic) with, and as a part of, a great body of similar facts, from which it will be impossible to abstract or distinguish those of individual firms or corporations. Individual statements are necessary for the formation of aggregate results. If necessary you may state that examination of the returns is not permitted for any private purpose, nor does the Department allow access to them for other than public uses."[97] Only businesses with annual productions over $500.00 were to be included, exempting small mechanical shops and household manufacturers. Total capital invested in the specified industry was to be listed as an aggregate of the real estate, working capital and personal monies invested.

Of particular interest to those planning secession, should have been the inventories of *"Raw Materials"* also included in Schedule No. 5. "By 'raw material' is meant the articles used for the production of a manufacture." Complicating the chore of the census taker was the reminder

---

[93] Pg. 23, schedule 4, point 2

[94] Page 23, schedule 4, point 3

[95] Page 24, schedule 4, point 44

[96] Page 24, schedule 5

[97] Pg 24, Schedule No. 5

that the "article produced or manufactured by one establishment may be the raw material of another; as copper ore, the article produced by the miner, is the raw material of the copper smelter; or pig iron, the article produced at the furnace, is the raw material used at the forge wherein it becomes blooms—the raw material for the rolling mill. Hides are the raw material for the tanner; while leather, the article he produces, is the raw material in the manufacture of boots and shoes." This latter point, or actually lack of this lastly mentioned raw material, leather, and the footwear necessary to a mobile army of 1863, led to the clash at Gettysburg, Pennsylvania. Confederate troops, with a deficit of boots, foraged toward a shoe factory at Chambersburg, Pennsylvania, and encountered Union troops, with much better access to leather footwear.

Interestingly, certain types of business were noted to not require, *raw material.* Examples, mentioned in the instructions to the Assistant enumerator, were quarry operations and mining. Again, of strategic interest to North and South, was the quantity of these raw materials used in the given industry. These details were to be listed in the "usual mode and terms of expressing the weights, measurement, or amount of the articles when bought and sold, as pounds of tallow, bales of cotton, reams of paper, tons or bushels of coal, bushels or barrels of salt, pounds of sole, and sides or pounds of upper leather, &c; and you should precede the amount with the initial letters of such terms, as 'T' for ton, 'B' bales, 'Bush' bushels, 'Bls.' For barrels, &c."[98]

Figure 21 - Camp Life in the West— Go West, Young Man, Go West! A great recruiting poster.

Leslie's pg. 256 Chapter 12

---

[98]Pg. 26, Schedule 5, points 4,5,6

Chapter Eleven - Working Up Steam

During the census taking efforts, a special emphasis was placed on the extremely important natural resource, coal. In addition to clarifying the units of mining product, as bushels or tons, the type of coal produced was very important to specify. As the major fuel source of the era, in addition to wood and water power, "great care" was to be taken in the listing of coal as "Charcoal, anthracite, bituminous, or cannel coal."[99] For proposed military action, this could be a significant detail.

Each of these types of coal was important in its own right. Despite use by the Hopi Indians in what would become the Southwest area of the United States, in the 1300s, this concentrated power source would not become central to industrialization until the development of the steam engine. By the 1740s the first commercial coal mines were established in Virginia. Unfortunately for the future Confederacy, the coal of the southern states was almost exclusively located in the vulnerable Richmond area coal fields.[100] In addition to the use of coal for the generation of steam for trains, ships, and in many manufacturing industries, significantly coal was increasingly used in weapons factories.[101]

In the antebellum and civil war years, the most prevalent types of coal were lignite which found mainly in the Trans-Mississippi River area and is least efficient as power source, compared to the other coals, bituminous, also known as "soft coal," and anthracite. The bituminous type was more energy dense than lignite and was fortunately mined in areas East of the Mississippi, such as in Kentucky, Ohio, Illinois, Pennsylvania and Virginia. Unfortunately, for the Confederacy, anthracite was the most energy efficient of coals and was least in quantity and found chiefly in Pennsylvania.[102] It was also anthracite coal which powered the first successful steam engine in 1825 at the Phoenixville Iron Works in Pennsylvania.

As this physical steam built up pressure in American industry, emotional steam continued to build up in the American Congress. This steam was to be vented in secession. The fuel of slavery, boilers of economy, pressure of states' rights propelled the United States into the disunited states. Release of steam was attempted. Some compromises were seen to delay the explosion. However, by the winter of 1860-61, secession was the explosion resulting from rivets popping in the ship of State.

---

[99] Pg 26, point 4

[100] Virginia Division of Mineral Resources, vol. 47, pg. 34

[101] http://fossil.energy.gov/education/energylessons/coal/coal_history.html

[102] http://www.fossil.energy.gov/education/energylessons/coal/gen_coal.html

In an interesting synopsis of the antebellum period, "Secession is not intended to break up the present government, but to perpetuate it. We do not propose to go out by way of breaking up or destroying the Union as our fathers gave it to us, but we go out for the purpose of getting farther guarantees and security for our rights, not by a convention of all the Southern states, nor by Congressional trick, which have failed in times past, and will fail again. But our plan is for the Southern states to withdraw from the Union for the present, to allow amendments to the Constitution to be made guaranteeing our just rights; and if the Northern states will not make those amendments, by which these rights shall be secured to us, than we must secure them the best way we can. This question of slavery must be settles now or never. The country has been agitated seriously by it for the past twenty or thirty years. It has been a festering sore upon the body politic; and many remedies having failed, we must try amputation, to bring it to a healthy state. We must have amendments to the Constitution, and if we can not(sic) get them we must set up for ourselves." So stated the address of commissioners sent to Maryland from Mississippi on December 9th, 1860.[103]

The political movement of secession was based upon the premise that sovereign parties to a Contract are themselves the only judges whether the contract is violated and they absolved from it; "a declaration which set utterly at naught the prescribed authority of the Supreme Court to decide upon the constitutionality of any state or national law, and which thus showed the radically destructive purposes of those who avowed it." Furthermore, it was felt that the release of this steam in the act of secession would not result in an actual explosion. "The seceders(sic) also looked to the accomplishment of their purposes with impunity, by reason of the support, or at least the protection, of a powerful party—the well-disciplined rank and file of the pure Democratic party—in the free states. And these expectations were not entirely without reason, Many men still looked upon secession as a mere political movement, the last, most desperate effort of the slavery propaganda to retain its control of the notional government, the culmination of the great game of bluff and brag which that party had so successfully played for so many years. This, indeed, was doubtless the original purpose of the greater number of those who took part in the secession movement."

The boiler did give way. While the southerners had hopes that they would suffer little from scalding, relative to their northern neighbors, they were wrong. Initially, in the first concussion of this blow out, the northern economy was soaked and burnt. In just days, " the North fell from a state of remarkable and soundly-based prosperity. The South owed the North a sum estimated by competent persons at three hundred millions of dollars; and, even supposing that this was one third too large, the consequences of a refusal to pay, or even a temporary withholding so vast a sum, must needs be hopeless derangement and sudden ruin. The secessionists from the beginning looked only to success, regardless of the nature of the means they used and the consequences of their conduct to others; and this sum was in a great measure withheld, for the double purpose of crippling those to whom it was due, and using it to pay the

---

[103] Introduction to Harper's Illustrated History of the Civil War, 1869, pg. 24.

expense of war with them".[104] What goes around comes around.

Figure 22 - Alexander H. Stephens, as Vice President of the Confederacy, seated 3rd from left.

Harper's pg. 210

---

[104] Introduction Harper's Illustrated History of Civil War, pg 24.

Chapter Twelve - Georgia on My Mind

In further irony, focusing on the increasing tensions between slave owning states and the North, A.H. Stephens delivered a moving speech in the Hall of the House of Representatives of Georgia. This gentleman, Alexander Hamilton Stephens, was an eloquent voice for the Southern cause. Born in Wilkes County, Georgia on February 11, 1812, orphaned by age fifteen, and initially educated for the ministry, Stephens became an attorney. After a sickly childhood and personal struggles, he exhibited his forthright character in returning the monetary funds that had been paid by the Georgia Educational Society in the pursuit of his education for the ministry. As a lawyer, Stephens supported his home state in the turbulent antebellum decades. In 1836, he began his illustrious political career with his election to the Georgia House of Representatives.

As a loyal southerner, yet ethical gentleman, Stephens desired to follow legal methods to achieve his aims. He continued to serve in the state house until 1842, at which time he was elected to the Georgia State Senate. Only one year later he moved on to the national political scene upon his election to the United States House of Representatives. Similarly to many other notables of the Confederacy, he ran as a Whig. There he continued to labor for the south, through legal means. This effort included his vociferous opposition to the Mexican War, support of the annexation of Texas, and active support of the Compromise of 1850.

In 1852, upon the nomination of General Winfield Scott for President of the U.S., Stephens, along with fellow Southern Whigs, diverged from the northern faction of the party. His support was given to the campaign of Daniel Webster, after Scott denied support of the Compromise of 1850. Again, loyal to the South, Stephens joined the Democratic Party and continued to lobby for southern interests in Congress. Working through his legal channels, he supported the Kansas-Nebraska Act, which was successfully enacted in 1854. Still feeling that the interests of Georgia could be bettered within the legal bounds of the United States, he repeatedly stated his objections to the secession of the southern states. While opposing the secession of Southern states as a consequence of the election of Abraham Lincoln to the Presidency of the United States, Stephens felt that the time had not yet come for separation. He did recognize that the election was legal, in line with the U.S. Constitution, and that, "If he violates the Constitution, then will come our time to act. Do not let us break it because, forsooth, he may. If he does, that is the time for us to strike. I think it would be injudicious and unwise to do this sooner." With comments that soon would be strangely ironic, "I do not anticipate that Mr. Lincoln will do any thing (sic) to jeopardy our safety or security." While feeling that the President, "is bound by the constitutional checks which are thrown around him, which at this time renders him powerless to do any great mischief. This shows the wisdom of our system. The President of the United States is no emperor, no dictator; he is clothed with no absolute power. He can do nothing unless he is backed by power in Congress.

The House of Representatives is largely in the majority against him. In the Senate he will also be powerless. There will be a majority of four against him."[105]

Furthermore, "Why then, I say, should we disrupt the ties of this Union when his (Lincoln's) hands are tied, when he can do nothing against us." Stephens then admitted that while, he did not agree with immediate secession, he did feel such action was justified if the U.S. Legislature nullified the Fugitive Slave Act, or violated states' rights as set forth in the Georgia Platform.

As the Census of 1860 verified, Stephens recognized the advances of the U.S. during the preceding ten years. He noted, "There are defects in our government, errors in administration, and shortcomings of many kinds, but, in spite of these defects and errors, Georgia has grown to be a great state. Let us pause here a moment. In 1850 there was a great crisis, but not so fearful as this, for of all I have ever passed through, this is the most perilous, and requires to be met with the greatest calmness and deliberation."

"There were many among us in 1850 zealous to go at once out of the Union, to disrupt every tie that binds us together. Now do you believe, had that policy been carried out at that time, we would have been the same great people that we are to-day? It may be that we would, but have you any assurance of that fact? Would you have made the same advancement, improvement, and progress in all that constitutes material wealth and prosperity that we have?

"I noticed in the Comptroller General's report that the taxable property of Georgia is $670,000,000 and upward, an amount not far from double that it was in 1850. I think I may venture to say that for the last ten years the material wealth of the people of Georgia has been nearly, if not quite doubled. The same may be said of our advance in education, and everything (sic) that marks our civilization. Have we any assurance that, had we regarded the earnest but misguided patriotic advice, as I think, of some of that day and disrupted the ties which bind us to the Union, we would have advanced as we have? I think not. Well, then, let us be careful now before we attempt any rash experiment of this sort. I know that there are friends, whose patriotism I do not intend to question, who think the Union a curse, and that we would be better off without it. I do not so think; if we can bring about a correction of these evils which threaten—and I am not without hope that this may yet be done—this appeal to go out, with all the provisions for good that accompany it I look upon as a great, and , I fear, a fatal temptation.

When I look around and see our prosperity in every thing (sic), agriculture, commerce, art, science, and every department of education, physical and mental, as well as moral advancement, and our colleges, I think, in the face of such an exhibition, if we can, without the loss of power, or any essential right or interest, remain in the Union, it is our duty to ourselves and to the posterity to –let not too readily yield to this temptation—do so."[106] Unfortunately, later in the same speech, A.H. Stephens did state his support of secession, not based on the placement of Lincoln in the Presidency, but if the Fugitive Slave Law was repealed or modified or if Lincoln's policies were carried out in violation of principles stated in the Georgia

---

[105]Harper's Pictorial History of the Civil War, 1866 pg. 19

[106]Pg 20, 1860, Harper's Pictorial History of the Civil War

Platform. In the vernacular of the time, Stephens stated that, " if those aggressions therein provided for take place, I say to you and to the people of Georgia, keep your powder dry, and let your assailants then have lead, if need be."

When Stephens made this address to the Georgia State Legislature in November of 1860, he reiterated this opposition before the Georgia convention on secession two months later. When his state did move to separate from the north, he employed his legal expertise to aid in the formation of the Confederate States of America. As a reflection of his public standing and loyalty to the South, he was elected as the Vice President of the Confederacy. He also was honored with his likeness on the $20.00 Confederate bill.

Stephen's militia minded directive was much more difficult for his fellow Southerners to accomplish, than for Northerners. As defined in the Census of this same year, lead mining was centered in the Upper Mississippi River Valley. Lead ore deposits were mined in southern Wisconsin, north eastern Iowa, and particularly in northwestern Illinois. Galena, Illinois, hometown of soon to be Lieutenant General, and future President, Ulysses S. Grant, was named for the underlying "Galena" deposit which supplied almost 90% of lead in the antebellum United States.[107] Not only was the military significance of these deposits acknowledged, this area contained the earliest commercial mines in the country. To assure a ready lead supply for the U.S. military, lead and copper mines on public lands were reserved from sale but were leased to developers. Initially, the Federal Government was to receive 10 % of the lead produced as rent, but later decreased the rent to six per cent. This relationship apparently went over like a lead balloon.

Unfortunately, Secretary of the Treasury, William H. Crawford found that these leases were so, "insufficiently productive of revenue, President James Monroe transferred the function to the War Department, November 29,1821, where it would be managed for the benefit of the army's demand for rifle shot.[108] Interestingly, the Secretary of War overseeing these mines was John C. Calhoun. He delegated this duty to the Ordnance Department where Col. George Bomford faced the same issue of insufficient funding that the Secretary of the Interior faced with his Census efforts. As Chief of Ordnance, Bomford (appropriately named), began to detail army officers to supervise the mines in lieu of more expensive civilian monitors.

Ironically, Census Assistants were also at times army officers, especially in the lightly populated areas of the west. In the case of lead mines, these officers were unofficially called, "Superintendents, U.S. Lead Mines" or "U.S. Mineral Agents." By December 22, 1845, President James K. Polk, recommend that this arrangement be terminated, again due to more expense to manage mines than was generated by the leases. The mines were returned to the

---

[107]Galena Area Lead Mining: Local Mining History,

http://jove.geol.niu.edu/faculty/fischer/429_info/429trips/Vinegar_Hill/Webpages/Mining_Hist ory.html

[108]Records of the Bureau of Land Management, 49.5 Records of the War Department Relating to Lead Mines 1824-47

Government Land Office by law on July 11, 1846. Despite the poor cost effectiveness of the lead leases, the Confederacy was without such access to lead, as the former major supplier, Great Britain, had depleted most of its deposits by this time and the cost and hazards of imports due to blockading made such supply difficult. The deposits remaining in Great Britain were also of lesser quality than that under the Union States.

Southern lead deposits were vulnerably centered in western Virginia. Unlike the Northern deposits, the deposit of Virginia was tapped almost exclusively in one location, Austinville. There, the political whims of the populace also influenced production of the vital lead for the Confederacy. [109] While Virginia remained the major mineral-producing state in the South, both antebellum and during the actual War, the mountainous population did not have universal loyalty to the Confederacy. This resulted in "a notoriously unreliable workforce where absenteeism and desertion were common."[110]

Fortunately, the southern United States was in a better position in regard to the supply of gunpowder to "keep dry." This essential material for the success of the proposed military maneuvers was traditionally a mixture of potassium nitrate, charcoal and sulfur. While various recipes, chiefly varying in the proportion of each ingredient, have been used over centuries, potassium nitrate is the most essential ingredient.[111] This ingredient has been traditionally called "saltpeter" and is essential in that it serves as an oxygen source for the rapid burning of the charcoal. Sulfur is not absolutely necessary but mainly functions to lower the temperature needed to ignite the mixture. The basic ratio of the ingredients in traditional black powder as referred to in 1860 Georgia, would be 75% saltpeter, by weight, mixed with 15% softwood charcoal, and 10% sulfur. Other proportions of the ingredients would be used in other applications, such as blasting in quarries. The charcoal was not to be pure carbon as the remaining cellulose, not completely decomposed, served as fuel for the small explosions to occur within the weapon and, significantly, charcoal has a lower temperature required for auto-ignition than pure carbon.[112]

Fortunately for troops or hunters in the field, gunpowder made with saltpeter defined as potassium nitrate, as opposed to other nitrate sources such as sodium nitrate, tends to be less affected by moisture or humidity. Fascinatingly, muzzleloaders have discharged after decades of wall hanging while still loaded with this old powder. Also a process called "Corning" helped to make the powder more stable. In this way, black powder would be compressed into "corns" or "mill cakes" or grains with the addition of moisture. This dampness also served to decrease flammable, explosive dust during the manufacturing process. Corned gun powder also ignites more thoroughly and evenly, resulting in less residual powder and more effective power for

---

[109] Virginia Division of Mineral Resources, vol. 47, pg .34

[110] Virginia Division of Mineral Resources, vol. 47, pg .38.

[111]Buchanan, Brenda J., ed.(2006), Gunpowder, Explosives and the State: A Technological History, Aldershot: Ashgate, ISBN 0754652599.

[112]Black Powder Recipes (http://www.musketeer.ch/blackpowder/recipe.html), Ulrich Bretscher

each shot.[113] Ironically, even with this advancement from the middle-ages, literature from 1885 documented, "Gunpowder is such a nervous and sensitive spirit, that in almost every process of manufacture it changes under our hands as the weather changes."[114]

The climate of the nation was exhibiting a similar "nervous and sensitive spirit." Despite the more humid southern states, the powder was quite easily mixed from more universally available components. Wood charcoal was from soft wood trees, such as alder, buckthorn or willow. Saltpeter was harvested from diverse areas and the southern states generally did not face gunpowder shortages. Other alternatives had been investigated, including a U.S. patent obtained by Christian Frederick Schonbein, from Basle, Switzerland, in 1846. His plan was an "Improvement in Preparation of Cotton-Wool and Other Substances as Substitutes for Gunpowder," in which acids were combined with cotton-wool to form cellulose nitrate.[115]

While gun powder reserves were not sufficient in the Confederacy at the onset of war, such creative substitutes were not necessary, even though Union blockade did remarkably hinder importation from overseas. While it is believed that the South had only one month of gunpowder reserve at the onset of War, major deposits were well known and well used in western Virginia since prerevolutionary war years.[116] Fortunately, also, this resource was regenerating continually. While also supplying a lion's share of salt, iron, coal and lead to the Southern cause, Virginia remained the "major mineral-producing state in the South both before and during the Civil War."[117] As opposed to other mineral mining operations, saltpeter, also called niter, was supplied from caves and even under outbuildings. Scattered, "highly decentralized (a trait common to niter production throughout the Confederacy)," production facilities were not easy to locate and were "never the principal target of Union attacks, although several such facilities were threatened and even destroyed from time to time during Federal invasions."[118]

Found literally lying on the floor of caves throughout the more mountainous region of Virginia, the nitrate deposits were felt originally to be based on bat waste known as guano. However, research by Hill in 1981 revealed that "nitrifying bacteria in surface soils oxidizing organic nitrogen to nitrate which is then dissolved by percolating groundwater and carried

---

[113]Kelly, Jack (2004), Gunpowder: Alchemy, Bombards, & Pyrotechnics: The History of the Explosive that Changed the World, Basic Books, ISBN 0465037186.

[114] C. E. Munroe (1885) ─Notes on the literature of explosives no. VIII", Proceedings of the US Naval Institute, no. XI, p. 285.

[115]http:www.businesshistory.com/ind.-weapons.php

[116] Virginia Minerals, vol. 47, No. 4, pg. 38

[117]Geology and History of Confederate Saltpeter Cave Operations in Western Virginia, Robert C. Whisonant, in Virginia Minerals, vol. 47, no. 4, Nov. 2001, pg 1

[118]Pg 2

downward to anaerobic soils and rock interstices where it is reduced to ammonium. If caverns are present, the infiltrating waters move toward the caves due to a moisture-density gradient within the bedrock created by evaporation at the cave air-bedrock interface. Upon reaching the cave boundary, the ammonium in solution is oxidized to nitrate with the help of nitrifying bacteria. If porous cave sediment is in contact with bedrock, seeping groundwater will be drawn to the surface of the sediment where evaporation and bacterial action cause nitrate concentration."[119] This theory also helps to explain why saltpeter caves were so prevalent in the Southeastern states. In other areas, temperature, humidity, and other variables of the environment would cause the nitrate to dissolve and evaporate.

The harvesting of saltpeter was, unlike the chemistry involved in its creation, relatively straightforward and feasible for even small operators. Workers, known as "peter monkeys", dug "peter dirt" from cave floors, or even from under outhouses, brought the earth to fresh water containing barrels, vats or tubs, where the nitrate was leeched from the dirt and mixed with wood ashes. These ashes supplied potassium salts, which would displace magnesium and calcium from the leech water. This concoction was filtered through cheesecloth and boiled in the open, similar to making maple syrup. When this water was evaporated, crystals of potassium niter or nitrate remained. Research by Powers in 1981, documented the ability of three men using this technique to be able to produce 100-200 pounds of essential niter in three days.[120]

While these steps were relatively safe, the next step in the production of gunpowder was much more dangerous. The saltpeter would be transported to gunpowder mills, the largest in the Confederacy being located in Augusta, Georgia. There 45 pounds of niter was mixed with 6 pounds of sulfur and 9 pounds of charcoal, producing 60 pound batches that would go through the corning process, resulting in grains of varying size to be used as gunpowder.[121]

---

[119] Virginia Minerals, No 4, pg 35

[120] Virginia Minerals, No 4, pg 37

[121] Virginia Div of Minerals, vol. 47, pg 38

SALT VALLEY.

Figure 23 - Salt Valley area of Western Virginia——Rich Iron and Lead and Gun Powder Resources for the Confederacy

Harper's 682

Figure 24 - Saltville, Virginia Vital Natural Resources Source for the South

Harper's pg. 682

To ensure a steady supply of niter, the Confederacy created a niter corps, within the Ordnance Department and later established a Niter and Mining Bureau, which by 1864 included six chemists, and six assistants. These men oversaw 14 mining and niter districts, with about 29 percent of the saltpeter produced in the Commonwealth of Virginia.[122] With $1.00 to $1.50 per pound paid for niter, a cottage industry also helped keep the Confederate military well supplied throughout the War. While pay was 60 cents per day at Horner's powder works, the workers were exempted, as essential employees for the war effort, from military service. While most workers were free men, some slave labor was employed. In comparison, in mid-nineteenth century wages, weavers, dyers, and warpers (sic) in Philadelphia averaged five dollars per week, spoolers fifty cents to one and a half dollars and bobbin winders just over one dollar per week.[123]

Ironically, it has been noted by Powers in 1981, "had the majority of the nation's saltpeter caves been located north of the Mason-Dixon Line rather than south, the war would certainly have ended much sooner."[124] If Stephens and colleagues had foreseen this advantage, and

[122]Virginia Div. of Minerals, vol 47, pg 38

[123]American Manufacturers, pg. 316

[124]Virginia Div. of Minerals, vol 47, pg 40

79

actually seceded after the 7th census in 1850, rather than after the 8th census, only ten years later, the enemy was not only much smaller, but also much less industrialized. Southern strengths remained more or less stable, while Northern strengths increased exponentially in these few short years.

Even as the cotton industry increased the Southern wealth, the actual manufacturing of cotton products was chiefly outside the Southern states and placed the wealth in jeopardy of embargo, tariffs, and Civil War. In the year 1825, Eli Whitney, the fabled "inventor of the saw gin, and one of the most eminent mechanics of his age, died."[125] He only reached the age of fifty-nine and fortunately could not have fully realized the impact his invention had in dividing the country. In an historic perspective, this one man may have contributed more to the Civil War than practically any other individual. Without the cotton gin, slave labor and abolition, tariff issues, and States Rights would have been less contentious.

Whitney did live to see cotton crop production increase in the United States from "about five millions of pounds to two hundred and fifteen millions, and the exports of the article augmented from less than half a million pounds to one hundred and forty-two and a quarter millions of pounds, the result in no small degree of the benefits conferred upon the planter by his invention."[126] Also, by 1825, the actual amount grown was estimated to be two hundred and fifty-five millions of pounds annually and the price per pound ranged from 11 cents to thirty-two cents per pound. The wide fluctuation related to speculation in the cotton market.

While cotton goods were manufactured in the southern states, with 158 establishments listed in these states by 1860, the northern states far outdistanced their neighbors. In just the states of the Northeast, Maine, New Hampshire, Vermont, Massachusetts, Rhode Island, and Connecticut, 570 similar "establishments" existed. In addition, Western States, Ohio, Indiana, Illinois, Missouri, Kentucky, and Utah contained 22 and the Middle States, consisting of New York, Pennsylvania, New Jersey, Delaware, Maryland and the District of Columbia, contained 333 more. In terms of capital investment, only approximately $9,436,221.00 was in the south, out of total U.S. capital investment of over $98,000,000. As a microcosm of pre-war differences, and in graphic terms of southern manufacturing deficits, only about 44,000,000 pounds of cotton was used in the south, while almost 284,000,000 pounds was used in Northeastern states, alone.

In addition, there were only 6,713 looms in the south, compared to almost 120,000 in the North. These looms were further defined in terms of spindles in operation. The south again ran only 290,000 versus almost, astronomically, 5,000,000 in the north. Surprisingly these cotton factories were at times huge physical plants, employing thousands of individuals. Also surprisingly, the work force was female dominant in a ratio of about 1.5 to 1. Even by modern standards these were significant numbers. One plant in Maine, at Cutts, or Factory Island, at the Falls of the Saco River, was completed in 1830. As the largest factory to that date ever constructed in the United States, it measured 210 feet long by 47 feet wide, seven stories high,

---

[125] American Manufacturers, pg. 298

[126] American Manufactures, pg. 298

and contained $200,000 in machinery. In the same year the entire facility burned to the ground, only to be rebuilt under a successive company. The southern states were at a significant disadvantage and this did not improve over the decades.

Even a non-statistician, and non-census taker, William Tecumseh Sherman, could see these disadvantages. Of course, under his scorched earth policy of splitting the Confederacy with his march across Georgia, he personally did contribute to devastating the southern economy. This was not without, a personal, and ironical, forewarning on Christmas Eve of 1860. "The North can make a steam engine, locomotive or railway car; hardly a yard of cloth or a pair of shoes can you make. You are rushing into war with one of the most powerful, ingeniously mechanical and determined people on earth—right at your doors. You are bound to fail"[127]

This advice was surely not easy for southern ears to hear and many of these advances had taken place only in the preceding decade. This direct, if not immodest prophecy, was not as foreseeable at the time of the 7th census as at the time of the 8th census.

---

[127] The Civil War, Bruce Catton, pg. 399

Figure 25 - General William Tecumseh Sherman

Harper's pg. 597

THE POWDER-BOAT LOUISIANA.

Figure 26 - Powder-Boat –Louisiana" bound for Federal troops.

Hit at 830 yards by Confederates from Ft. Fisher on 12/23/64 Blew up with 4 separate explosions, felt to be advantageous, due to packing of fuses and powder appropriately which prevented one "instantaneous explosion" of the 235 TONS of gun powder on board.

Harper's pg. 725

Figure 27 - Dangerous Job—Moving Gunpowder During Bombardment at Ft. Sumter.

Harper's pg. 59

Figure 28 - Creative Use of Explosives

"Infernal Machine Designed by the Confederates to Destroy the Federal Flotilla in the Potomac Discovered by Captain Budd of the Steamer "Resolute." ""Two large eighty-gallon oil casks, perfectly watertight, acting as buoys, connected by twenty-five fathoms of three-and-a-half-inch rope, buoyed with large squares of cork, every two feet secured to casks by iron handles. A heavy bomb of boiler iron, fitted with a brass tap and filled with powder, was suspended to the casks six feet under water. On top of the cask was a wooden box, with fuse in a gutta-percha tube. In the centre (sic) of the oak was a platform with a great length of fuse coiled away, occupying the middle of the cask."" July 7th, 1861

Leslie's pg. 163

THE WAR IN VIRGINIA—EXPLOSION OF A TORPEDO UNDER THE "COMMODORE BARNEY," ON JAMES RIVER, AUGUST 4th, 1863

KEY OF THE FORT MOULTRIE MAGAZINE.

Figure 30 - Iron-key to victory

Harper's pg. 27

FORGING A BLOOM.

Figure 31 - Forging the Iron for Victory Harper's Pictorial History of the Civil War, first edition, vol. 1, 1866, pg 259

FORGING A PLATE.

Figure 32 - Forging A Plate **Harper's Pictorial History, pg. 259**

As the North became increasingly industrialized, the northern economy became more dependent on iron. In the decade between the Seventh and Eighth Censuses, a considerable increase both in the number of Blast Furnaces and Rolling Mills occurred. The United States was believed to be the source of "inexhaustible resources" and "destined to become the source of supply for the world."[128] While Europe was felt to be likely depleted of capacity to produce a higher quality of iron, both the northern and southern United States took pride in their resources.

Specifically, England, Germany, and France had been traditionally superior iron producers. By the 1850s, however, the coals necessary for refining processes became more limited overseas. While Russia was a significant source of iron, the sources of ore were "so distant that it requires nearly two summers to reach a port of shipment."[129]

In a most unlikely manner, "The war has secured to the iron-masters of the United States a protection more reliable and stable than any protective tariff, and they can now proceed to extend their operations with confidence of permanency; and when they have supplied the home demand, they will have acquired skill and advantages that will enable them to compete successfully with other nations in foreign markets."[130] The southern states soon were considering themselves as a foreign market, relative to the Union. Earlier dissention, over proposed protective tariffs, prevented the inclusion of most iron as a protected item. The first set of tariffs, which were viewed as truly effective in the opinion of manufacturers of the day, was in place on the 30th of June, 1824. This "passage of this act produced much dissatisfaction and threats of retaliation both in England and the Southern States. At public meeting, resolutions to abstain from the use of every thing (sic) produced in the tariff states, and even from communication with them, with various propositions of a retaliatory kind were passed in Baldwin county, Georgia, and Barnwell district, South Carolina, and much excitement was manifested elsewhere." Interestingly, no tariff protection was included for manufacturers of glass, paper, or iron, except for "hammered bar iron."[131]

Census efforts well documented the increase in this iron industry. The wealth of iron lay under areas of the Union and under the future Confederacy. In the south the chief iron ore lay with coal, copper and even gold deposits in western Virginia, eastern Tennessee and extended through the mountainous band into Alabama. Southern furnaces, forges, hammers, and bloomeries sprang up relatively nearby. This area also supplied the necessary hardwoods,

---

[128] American Manufacturing, Production of Iron in the United States, pg. 812

[129] American Manufacturing, Production of Iron, pg. 812

[130] Am. Man. Prod of Iron, pg 812

[131] Am. Man. Prod of Iron, pg 812

chiefly hickory, oak, beech, and maple, which were used to create the charcoal used in iron processing. Unlike the charcoal needed in saltpeter manufacturing, which was preferably made from soft woods, the hardwood, hotter burning, was essential to melt the ore.[132] These hardwoods also produced much more charcoal than soft woods. In an early evaluation of these characteristics, Gerard Troost, in 1840, noted that hickory would yield 1,172 pounds of hardwood charcoal per cord burned, while white pine produced only about 455 pounds per cord.[133]

Very impressively, research by Williams 1994, Dunaway 1996, and Davis 2000, calculated that, "The average nineteenth-century blast furnace, producing 2 tons of iron a day, therefore consumed about 300 acres of mature timberland a year."[134]

While the Union had greater iron reserves, much of this area was relatively far removed from the industrializing centers. This was not really as much of a challenge for the North due to ability to move ore via the Great Lakes, sizable rivers and through the expanding railroad system. In the years between 1860 and 1885, one-third of this iron was used for construction of railways.[135] The South similarly did have rivers sufficient to supply necessary fresh water to power bellows, cool hot iron and help transport the product. Unfortunately, the South did not have the railroad infrastructure to transport the ore as easily. Also, the area was much more dependent on further iron processing in the North or overseas. This export tended to be through ports such as New Orleans, Natchez, or Mobile and placed almost the entire industry under the influence of blockade by the Federal Navy.

Of greatest importance to the development of the manifest destiny was the massive growth of railroads. The iron deposits of the southern shore of Lake Superior, carried over the Great Lakes, via the newly completed Michigan State Locks, more commonly known as the Soo Locks, were used in iron manufacturing which contributed to the nearly 4 fold increase in the railroad network in the decade between the 1850 and 1860 censuses. The Locks made possible direct transport, without a portage, around the 1.25 miles of the rapids of the St. Mary's River at the eastern end of Lake Superior.[136] Completed in June 1855, iron ore flowed chiefly into the steel mills of Ohio, Pennsylvania and New York. In return , the iron ore production became more profitable and efficient via these newly constructed rail routes and more rails were laid into the ore bearing areas.

Even though the South enjoyed fairly large iron manufacturing sites such as the Bumpass Cove mines, Embree Iron Works and Tellico Iron Company in eastern Tennessee and Estill Furnace of Kentucky, large furnaces were located in northern Georgia, Alabama and scattered in other southern states. Unfortunately for the owners of furnaces in some Upland locations, by

---

[132] Donald Davis, Southern United States, An Environmental History, pg. 150.

[133] Donald Davis, Southern United States, An Environmental History, pg. 151

[134] Davis, pg 151

[135] http.//www.geo.msu.edu/geogmich/ironsteel.html pg. 1

[136] http://www.geo.msu.edu/geogmich/ironsteel.html

the 1860 census some production was waning, partially due to the fact that, "Upland water routes proved insufficient for the transport of large quantities of iron to major southern river ports."[137] Unfortunately, the railroad network of the southern states was not nearly of the quantity or quality of the northern states.

While iron was produced in traditional blast furnaces, much was produced in the smaller bloomery forges. These were often quite far flung, consisting of "a large hammer and anvil, both of which were usually made of iron and each weighed as much as 750 pounds. The fires of the forge were fueled by charcoal and continuously controlled by a stream of water that created blasts of air in the same manner as a bellows."[138]

Probably the most famous of the large southern iron producers was the Tredegar Iron Works in Richmond, Virginia. While the Confederacy had seized 135,000 guns from Federal arsenals located throughout the South at the onset of War, many were out of date. Unfortunately, the only facility for manufacturing rifles that existed in the south was destroyed by Union troops when the armory at Harper's Ferry was evacuated.[139]

It was obviously essential for the South to have access to weapons of all calibers rapidly. Some of the equipment for manufacture of fire-arms was salvaged from Harper's Ferry and sent

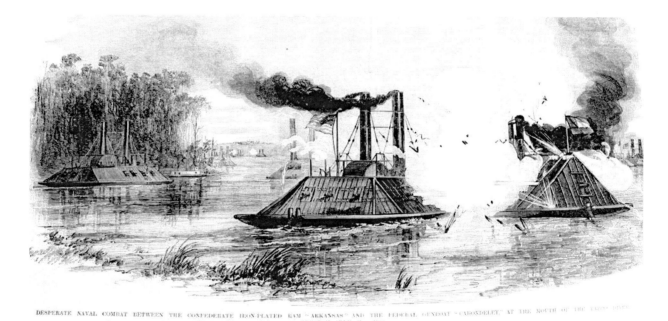

DESPERATE NAVAL COMBAT BETWEEN THE CONFEDERATE IRON-PLATED RAM "ARKANSAS" AND THE FEDERAL GUNBOAT "CARONDELET" AT THE MOUTH OF THE YAZOO RIVER, TUESDAY, JULY 15th, 1862.

Figure 33 Iron-plated Confederate Ram, *Arkansas* in Combat with Union Gunboat, *Carondelet* on July 15th, 1862

Leslie's pg. 224

[137] Southern United States: An Environmental History, pg 154

[138] Southern United States: An Environmental History, pg. 151

[139] The Civil War, Bruce Catton, pg. 407

Figure 34 - Mortar Boats Under Construction

Harper's pg. 203

Figure 35 - "Iron Bluffs" and Iron Clad Boats

Leslie's 224

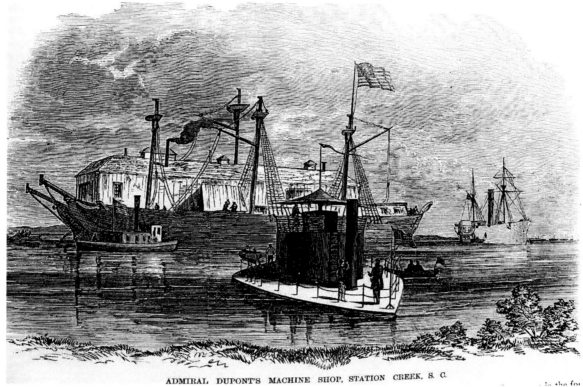

ADMIRAL DUPONT'S MACHINE SHOP, STATION CREEK, S. C.

Figure 36 - Portable Machine Shop, Station Creek, S.C.

Leslie's pg 463

to Richmond, Virginia and Confederate agents were sent to Europe to seek additional weapons.[140]

The manufacture of necessary iron products, particularly furnaces for smaller iron works, "projectiles, gun carriages, plates for ironclads, wheels and axels for railway rolling stock," were conducted at Tredegar. The plant produced the largest quantity of cannon, unfortunately all muzzle loaders, for the South, iron plate for the iron clad, CSS Virginia and rails of the deficient Confederate area railroads. There, the antebellum owner, and West Point graduate, Joseph Reid Anderson, continued to serve as the civilian manager.[141]

In addition to being the Confederate capital, home to the huge Tredegar works, Richmond was also the center of small arms production in the south. There the Virginia Arsenal was capable of producing 5,000 weapons per month. As reflected in the Censuses, laborers in this iron industry were a mixture of white, black, slave, and free, although there had been an effort to strike in 1847, reportedly not over wages but due to racists in the factory having objections to working with colored workers.[142] According to the Manufacturers of 1860, 1,115 men were employed at Virginia pig iron factories. Only 14 females were listed as employed in this industry in the entire state. This is particularly of interest when only 150 females were so employed

---

[140] Catton, pg 407

[141] Voices of the American Past, vol. 1 by Raymond Hyser, pg 238

[142] Voices of the American Past, vol. 1 by Raymond Hyser , pg 238

throughout the antebellum country, including the District of Columbia. Unfortunately the disparity between the wages for men and women were impressive, with the average wage for women listed at $6.86 PER MONTH in Virginia iron factories while men received an average wage of $12.76 per month. The only northern state listing this information in the American Manufacturers review of 1860 was Pennsylvania. There women were averaging $5.11 per month, while men averaged $21.65. Also of importance was the listing of only 9 employed women in the Pennsylvania pig iron producers, with 9,265 men employed in this state.[143]

In a practical sense, the Confederacy would have had a more stable labor force if more women had been employed in essential industries. Due to a smaller male population, southern men were in increased demand for the military when compared to northern men. Industrial owners and foremen had ongoing problems with man power. As men were conscripted into military service many left skilled positions. This constant drain on the manufacturing sector compounded material shortages, transportation issues and helped defeat the Confederacy. A complaint to the Assistant Quartermaster General stated this difficulty. While written in regard to the footwear industry, this statement reflected the problem as defined by Captain W.M. Gillaspie, in charge of a shoe factory in Richmond, "It takes fully one half of the time of one of my clerks and about as much of my own to attend to the detailing of men. I no sooner have a man trained and somewhat efficient than he is ordered to report to camp, and then after considerable delay I have his services replaced by a new one and an invalid, in most cases, who is one half the time in the Hospital and the other half not able to do much work."[144]

Just as the quartermaster general searched for able bodied men, materials for industry were conscripted. As an example, the Richmond shoe factory was forced to give up 66 out of 171 workers in January of 1865.[145] The footing was literally slippery for the South compared to the North. Just as the weapons manufacturing, iron production, and textile industries were deficient in the southern states and only becoming more lob sided, the shoe factories and leather handling facilities suffered as war lingered. In the case of tanneries, leather supplies were limited by the quartermaster general. This government department controlled raw materials for shoes for the

---

[143] American Manufactures, pg. 156

[144] Confederate Control of Manufacturing, vol. viii, no. 3, pg 248

[145] Confederate Control of Manufacturing, pg 248, footnote

Figure 37 - Horseshoeing, an essential service for both armies.

Leslie's pg. 400

Blacksmiths Department, Head-Quarters.

Figure 38 - Blacksmith's Department

Harper's pg. 485

army and harnesses for supply trains. The ordnance department sought the same hides for artillery harnesses and saddles.[146]

Similarly to the process of census questioning, the southern manufacturers were instructed to disclose otherwise confidential information to the central government. This was particularly galling to the independent, states' rights loving southerners. "The books of the concern should at all times be open to the inspection of the Enrolling Officer." Profits were also limited by the Confederate government to thirty-three and one third per cent in the textile industry and one third of the leather made from hides sold to the government.[147] By October 9, 1862, the Confederate Congress enabled President Jefferson Davis the authority to detail, through the quartermaster general, soldiers with experience as shoe makers to work in government shops. Up to 2000 such men were allowed extra pay. Through the control of hides, railroad transportation, and with tanneries attached to shoe factories, the private shoe manufacturers were placed in a precarious position. As war continued and the blockade of the south became more effective, the supply of leather sharply declined. Furthermore, as the Mississippi River fell under Union control, hides from Texas and Louisiana were sharply reduced. "A situation which was bad enough was made worse by the frequent gross carelessness or inefficiency of the officers and agents charged with preserving, collecting and shipping the hides, by the refusal of commissaries, who desired to make purchases with hides, to turn them over to the quartermasters, and, as demoralization grew, by the absence of proper control over distant quartermasters and agents, and by downright theft. Thousands of hides were kept out of the hands of the government by speculators, and evidence is not lacking that some minor officials themselves carried on private speculation in this much sought

---

[146] Confederate Control of Manufacturing, viii, no. 3, pg 239

[147] Confederate Control of Manufacturing, viii, no. 3, pg 245

Figure 39 - Five Locomotives Built by Federal Soldiers in Vicksburg, Mississippi

Leslie's pg. 369

Figure 40 - Mortar Roll your own

Leslie's pg. 308

Figure 41 - Iron breech reinforcement at Ft. Sumter

VMC

SIEGE OF VICKSBURG—GENERAL SHERMAN'S FIGHT WITH HAND GRENADES, JUNE 13th, 1863.

Figure 42 - Hand Grenades

Leslie' pg. 359

Figure 43 - Federal Mortar Boats in Action on the Mississippi River

Leslie's pg. 117

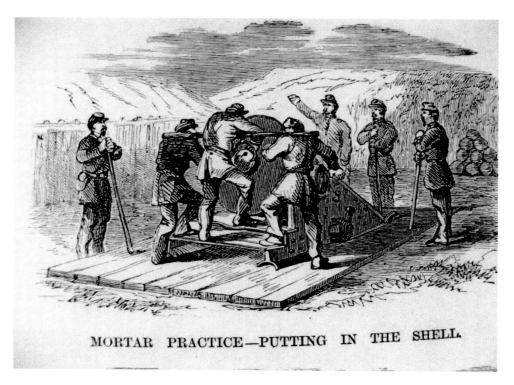

MORTAR PRACTICE—PUTTING IN THE SHELL.

Figure 44 - Mortar Practice

Leslie's pg. 177

BIG GUN
Commanding Channel

Figure 45 - Big Gun Cotton was at times used for protection on boats of gun emplacements

Harper's pg. 263

after commodity.[148] Interestingly, as the leather supply suffered, the Confederate government even tried to offset the shoe shortage by making foot wear with canvas tops.[149]

Actually during the pivotal battle at Gettysburg, the Confederate soldiers were hoping to procure additional shoes. The quartermaster with General Robert E. Lee's troops in Pennsylvania had requisitioned 20,000 pairs by telegraph. He was denied the footwear and ironically, conversely notified by the quartermaster general's office that, "I have been in anticipation of receiving stores from you and not to supply you."[150]

The textile industry suffered in a similar fashion, with at least one factory being refused a work detail unless the proprietors would sell their surplus material to the public at the same price as to the government. Obviously this pricing strategy would tremendously affect the profit margins. With precious little textiles returning to the South through the ever tightening blockade, the manufactures in the south could charge exorbitant rates for their goods. While the raw cotton remained generally plentiful in southern area of the Confederacy throughout most of the War years, the transport of the cotton over the "feeble railways," along with the lack of access to Northern or English markets placed the "King Cotton" industry into more of a pawn status.[151]

While the supply of cotton material far outdistanced the supply of wool in the south, the woolen industry was virtually monopolized by the Confederate government. Even with this control, by 1864 a large amount of trousers manufactured for the Southern army were all cotton. This shortage was much more severe than anticipated in that the "clip of 1863" from Texas did not make it over the Mississippi before the River fell to Union control. Even in the 1850 census this potential major problem was foreseeable. As Charles W. Ramsdell, of the University of Texas, so aptly stated in an address to a session of the American historical association and Mississippi valley historical association in Washington, DC in 1920, "It seems significant that the confederate government never devised nor even attempted to devise any civil machinery for the control or regulation of the factories upon whose production so much depended. The reason is clear: the supply of the army was regarded as solely a military problem. It was an army affair; leave it to the war department! Though an urgent, it was a temporary problem which would be over with the coming of peace. Perhaps the southerners disliked the idea of a permanent arrangement for interfering with private property rights; but probably they never thought of that at all. The military control which was gradually established was rigid, but partial, uneven, short-sighted. Its purpose was to get supplies for the army at as reasonable a cost as possible—to exploit the factories, not to develop them for the benefit of the community at large."[152]

---

[148] Confederate Control of Manufacturing, pg .247

[149] Confederate Control of Manufacturing, pg. 245

[150] Confederate Control of Manufacturing, pg. 246

[151] Confederate Control of Manufacturing, pg 239

[152] Confederate Control of Manufacturing , pg. 249

SPIKING THE GUNS OF FORT MOULTRIE BY MAJOR ANDERSON, BEFORE ITS EVACUATION. DECEMBER 26TH, 1860

Figure 46 - Spiking Guns of Fort Moultrie 12/26/1860 to Prevent use by the Enemy

Leslie's pg .55

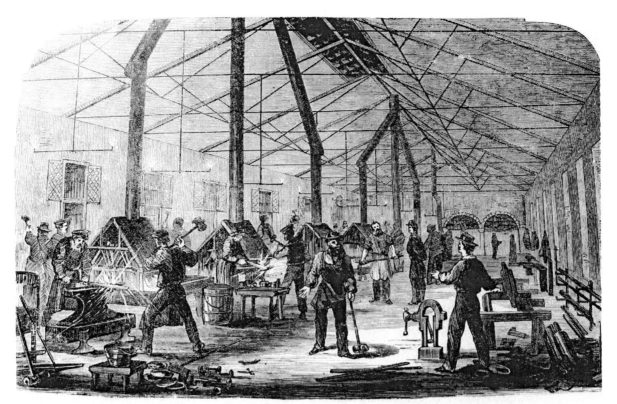

FORGING IRONWORK FOR GUN CARRIAGES AT THE WATERVLIET ARSENAL, WEST TROY, N. Y.

Figure 47 - Forging Ironwork For Gun Carriages at the Watervliet Arsenal, West Troy, N.Y.

Frank Leslie's History of the Civil War, first edition, pg. 78

THE SIEGE OF CHARLESTON—ORDNANCE DEPOT, MORRIS ISLAND, S. C.

Figure 48 - Ordnance Depot at Morris Island, S.C.

Leslie's pg. 475

Chapter Fourteen - King Cotton: Almost Deposed

As stated, near-sightedness, passion without logic, became tragic. Already, by the time of the 1850 census, the major agricultural products of the South were cotton, sugar cane, grain, and tobacco. Unfortunately the manifested destiny occurring between the 7th and 8th censuses was more manifest in the Northern than Southern United States. Much of this increase in the south also occurred in vulnerable Virginia, too close to the Northern capital to be comfortable. In addition to the location, location, location, the labor force was also vulnerable to the war in that almost 4 out of 5 slaves were owned by industrialists and totaled likely between 150,000 and 200,000 owned individuals working in these industries.

Comfort was to be taken in the southern states strong position in the global economy of the early 1800s. By the onset of War, these states accounted for approximately 70 per cent of the total United States exports and about 75% of these exports were cotton based. While a trickle of the exports were maintained during the war through the blockade by financial motivated fast blockade running ships, it is estimated that water transport, originating in the South fell by at least 90%. Compounding the problem, the privateers attempted an embargo on cotton shipments from their plantations to Europe. This was hoped to force the cotton dependent European countries to take sides with and formally recognize the Confederate States of America. Even with this ill proposed plan, the major amount of cotton to successfully leave the south went to its major trading partner, the northern states. With this illegal, very limited export, millions of bales were lost. Despite the efforts of U.S. Treasury agents actively attempting to purchase cotton from the south, the price fell, relative to gold in the south while increasing more than ten times the prewar price in the north. Supply and demand are forever at work.

Speculators also eyed the cotton market and plantation owners still suffered. To try to offset the lost sales, "cotton bonds" were issued but were of no real value due to astronomical inflation and lack of backing in gold. Issued as specie, these payments were not ultimately worth the paper they were printed on. As the bond or note owners often rushed to cash the paper in for actual goods, commodity prices rose and currency depreciated as well. While limited funds were raised overseas through the cotton futures market, this was generally unflavored by abolitionists in France, England and Germany, in particular. The U.S. government did everything possible to discourage this overseas support for the Confederacy. After the war, this displeasure was ultimately stated in Section 4 of the 14th Amendment to the U.S. Constitution. "neither the United States nor any State shall assume or pay any debt or obligation incurred in aid of insurrection or rebellion against the United States, or any claim for the loss or emancipation of any slave; but all such debts, obligations and claims shall be held illegal and void." Therefore, the southern states essentially lost cotton production, lost transportation by water and by rail, lost currency value, had no European recognition, and little vital resources such as medicine sources, clothing reserves, gold reserve or even coffee supply. This was foreseeable.

Already in 1850, the cotton textile manufacturers of the North exceeded those of the South by a total of approximately 971 to 123. Also, as reflected in the cotton sales, 641,240 bales were sold per the 1850 census with only 74,380 used in the southern mills. In a staggering comparison, the 213 cotton manufacturers in Massachusetts alone use 233,607 of these bales. Likewise the total yards of material produced in the south equaled about 359,514,960 out of a total national production of 763,678,407 yards. Also only 3705 mail employees were listed in the report of southern states, out of a total country wide work force of 33,150 men in these mills. This comparison should mention that Texas and Louisiana did not report statistics in this area, but that the amount of textiles produced in those states was minimal. Interestingly the number of women employed in these southern mills exceeded men. In the same report, 5,936 women were employed in the south out of a total of 59,136 women nation -wide. Sadly, the average female worker in a southern mill earned about $6.67 per MONTH while males earned approximately $14.88 per month. In the north the women did little better at about $7.50 per month and males made significantly better wages at about $17.87 per month.[153]

The significant states' rights advocates of the south also tried to restrict textiles produced in their home state from going to troops from other allied states. This effort was very pronounced in North Carolina where cloth manufacturers and tanneries did not want to share the state's production with other less fortunately blessed states.[154] Governor Vance was in charge of North Carolina at this vital time. By 1864, Confederate troops were increasingly desperate for shoes and clothing. Supplies were at times procured from captured Union stores and from dead Yankees. Unfortunately, as the shortages became more severe, "Quartermaster General Lawton instructed the post quartermaster at Raleigh to endeavor to get contracts for the bureau with the factories of North Carolina, if it could be done without coming into conflict with the state authorities."[155] Lawton was "informed that, owing to the scarcity of wool, the product of the woolen mills would not be shared, but that the confederate government was at liberty to make contracts with the cotton factories, since but few furnished the state more than one third of their output."[156] Even though this resistance is well documented, North Carolina was home to more than 1/3rd of textile manufacturers in the Confederacy east of the Mississippi River and likely was supplying half of the government procured cloth by 1864. Agents of the quartermaster general made rounds, more threatening than any census taker had ever undertaken. "'This,'" wrote Lawton's agent, 'looks to the factories as if everything was arranged in Richmond with special reference to forcing them into measures, and they so express themselves. It is not very material whether they are correct or not; but if they think so it makes it easier for me to make contracts.'" In addition, correspondence exists in the *Rebellion records,* in which Lawton related his frustrations with, "the troubles over the North Carolina factories, the growing

[153] Seventh Census, Chart A, pg. 154

[154] Confederate Control of Manufacturing , pg. 241

[155] Confederate Control of Manufacturing, pg. 241

[156] Pg. 242

scarcity of supplies available for the troops of other states, and the injustice and ill-consequences of the selfish policy followed by the state authorities."[157]

In 1860, of 158 cotton mills in the south, 38 were in North Carolina, 33 were in Georgia. In these latter 33 mills another almost 1/3rd of total southern production was produced. This was accomplished using 85,186 spindles and 2041 looms.[158] The actual value of these "cotton goods" in 1860 was listed as just over $8.1 million dollars, up from approximately $5.5 million just ten years earlier.[159] Northern states, however, experienced growth from $60 million in 1850 to over $108 million in 1860. The value in the northeastern states, Maine, New Hampshire, Vermont, Massachusetts, Rhode Island and Connecticut alone expanded from $43,785,990 to $79,359,900 during this same ten year period.

While Northern states did experience strife over resources during the war years, the Union troops remained much better clothed than Confederate soldiers. The industrial supply of uniforms in the northern states far exceeded the more decentralized, small cottage type of production more prevalent in the south. Initially southern troops were to be reimbursed or commutated, if they supplied their own clothing. This sum was initially to be $21.00 every six months and later increased to $25.00 every six months.[160] The women of the area, reviving "ancient household arts of spinning and weaving," could not meet the demand. If the soldier was unable to afford to buy his own attire, the Confederate secretary of war was to supply the uniform. After the autumn of 1861 almost all of the army uniforms were made in government run quartermaster's depots. After the autumn of 1862, the Confederate war department was legally responsible to supply all uniforms for noncommissioned officers and privates. While some of the textile goods, such as blankets, tents, and clothing were purchased outright by the Confederate government, many were donated by private individuals and by various charities.

Not only was there sizable profiteering in cotton products between sales to private individuals versus sales to the central government, there was also competition between the bureau of subsistence, the bureau of ordnance and the navy for the same materials. Supply did not meet demand on a practical and economically feasible manner. "Although competitive bidding between government agents was corrected to some extent by confining the contracts of each depot to a specified territory, competition by the general public was not eliminated. The manufacturers in many cases were finding larger profits in the rising public markets than in contracts with quartermasters, and either hesitated or declined outright to bind themselves to long term agreements at fixed prices."[161]

All wars are ultimately wars of attrition.

---

[157] Pg. 243

[158] Manufactures of the Southern States, 1860, pg. 808

[159] Manufactures of the Southern States, pg. 808

[160] The Mississippi Valley Historical Review, vol. viii, no. 3, pg. 232 by Charles W. Ramsdell

[161] Ramsdell, pg. 234

Figure 49 - Colored Infantry Bringing in Captured Guns Amid Cheers of the Ohio Troops at the Siege of Petersburg, VA

Leslie's pg. 438

Figure 50 - Loss of the Queen of the West

Harper's pg .450

Figure 51 - Unionist discovery of munitions intended for the Confederacy in Baltimore,

Leslie's pg. 225

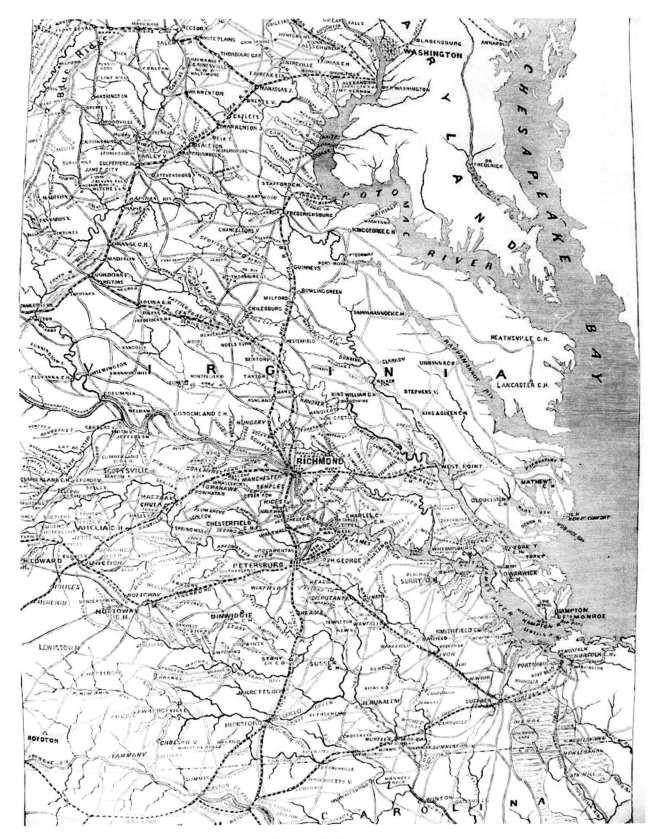

Figure 52 - Richmond-Crossroad of the Southern Railways

Harper's pg. 329

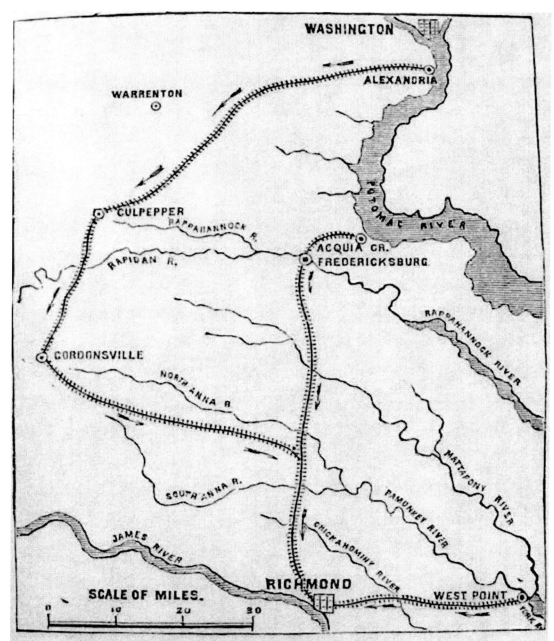

ROUTES TO RICHMOND.

This sketch illustrates the advantages, in point of distance, of the three proposed routes to Richmond. The first, abandoned by Burnside, assumes the basis of supply to be Alexandria. The second, proposed by him, assumes it to be at Acquia Creek. The third, that adopted by McClellan, places it at West Point.

Figure 53 - Capitol to capitol or capital to capital

Leslie's pg. 32

THE CONFEDERATE PRIVATEER STEAMER "ALABAMA" ("290"), CAPTAIN RAPHAEL SEMMES

Figure 54 - Most Famous Confederate Privateer or Blockade Runner, the *Alabama*.

Leslie's pg. 287

Chapter Fifteen - Creativity Inspired by Necessity

Attrition was the mother of invention in the southern states. While creativity of the North was reflected in industrialization, the South became increasingly creative in order to supply basic needs. The censuses reflect some of these manufacturing niches. In the south agrarian, organic products reigned. In the north, inorganic products reigned.

Always driven by profit, those unprofitable quickly failed. While cotton related gins and mills and plantations were very profitable in the warm southern states, another textile industry was less well known, more short lived, but theoretically suited to this area. As early as the seventeenth century, England hoped to gain advantage in textile manufacturing beyond basic cotton. The most glamorous and exotic of fabrics of the age were those made of silk. While generally linked to the far-east, very successful silk factories were located in Italy and France. The English developed the Trustee Garden in the city of Savannah in the colony of Georgia to experiment with potentially profitable plants. In order to develop this industry, experts immigrated to the colony from Italy and Germany.[162]

The cultivation of Mulberry trees was necessary as a food source for silk worms. The climate of Georgia was favorable to the trees but not to the essential worms. While fabric was made in the colony, even England's Queen Caroline had a dress made from this imported, colonial source in 1735, this success was short-lived.[163] The Queen had silk but the south had cotton as King. Temperamental silk production could not compete with cotton in profitability, simplicity, and hardiness. Basic slave labor was far more cost effective than the skilled labor necessary in silk production. Eli Whitney's development of the cotton gin at the end of the 18th century exponentially magnified this fact.

To aid in the success of the silk industry in the young United States, a duty of 30% was placed on imported silk under the Tariff of 1824. This was further raised by "an additional 5% on silk originating beyond the Cape of Good Hope, and of twenty per cent, on other manufactures of silk."[164] At that time silk became a very desirable commodity in the North and South. The northern states could help replace the cotton bales that were in shorter supply due to the hostilities, while the southern states could help replace the manufactured cotton fabrics that were limited due to the War.

---

[162] http://www.georgiaencyclopedia.org/nge/Article.jsp?id=h-2606

[163] http://www.georgiaencyclopedia.org/nge/Article.jsp?id=h-2606

[164] Manufactures of the Southern States, pg. 324

Figure 55 - Hiding Cotton in a Southern Swamp

Harper's pg. 443

BEADQUARTERS OF VINCENT COLLYER, SUPERINTENDENT OF THE POOR AT NEW BERNE N.C.—DISTRIBUTION OF CAPTURED CONFEDERATE CLOTHING TO THE CONTRABANDS

Figure 56 - Distribution of Confederate Captured Clothing to the Poor, New Berne, N.C.

Leslie's pg. 96

BUTCHERING AND DRESSING CATTLE FOR DISTRIBUTION TO THE FEDERAL ARMY.

Figure 57 - Cattle Processing for Meat and Leather for the Union Army

Frank Leslie's Illustrated History, pg. 331

Figure 58 - Cattle From Texas Transported Across Mississippi River

Harper's 449

While the manufacture of silk was over 4000 years old, the production of the basic silk fiber was relatively unchanged over the centuries. The origin of this surprisingly strong, light weight filament was China. There, legend states, a princess discovered that silkworms could be treated and unwound to develop into a thread that could be woven into precious fabric. She was deified for this creativity and lives in history as "Seine-Than", the "Goddess of Silk Worms." Her efforts also brought riches to China. Using the "silk road" which extended from the Far East to shipping ports on the Mediterranean Sea, the rare material became the envy of textile manufacturers. For hundreds of years the production techniques were secretively guarded but eventually the monopoly was broken as silk worm eggs and Mulberry tree seeds were smuggled out to the Roman Empire, via Persian monks by 522 A.D.[165]

By the 1700s England became the major silk producing center due to technological advancements in looms and fabric printing. In the continuing desire to derive profit from the New World colonies, the Old World industry was introduced into New England, Virginia, South Carolina, and Georgia. This set the stage for attempts at major silk production in both the North and the South by the Civil War. The very labor intensive process of extracting fibers from cocoons was not successful commercially in either area. Eggs were vulnerable to disease. If healthy, they needed to hatch, the larvae then being fed with Mulberry leaves, then go through the fourth molt, mount a twig, spin a cocoon, which is then treated with poison or steam to kill the encased pupae. This critical step prevents the metamorphosis which would result in the destruction of the encasing long, continuous filament.

Interestingly the technical name for this silk production is "sericulture." This term came from the name, "sericin." This glue or gum like substance combines two "continuous-filament fiber consisting of fibroin protein secreted from two salivary glands in the head of each

---

[165] History of Sericulture, pg 1

larvae."[166]

This adhesive was loosened by soaking in hot water and then "reeled" off the cocoon, made into yarns, rewound onto "reels" which were dried and then sent to looms. This industry was obviously tedious, vulnerable to loss at each stage and not conducive to effective use of slave labor. Cotton was hardier, much less labor intensive, even prior to the advent of the cotton gin, and more profitable by sheer volume.

Silk was not of strategic value to the warring factions. It did make beautiful flags, billowing above armies, or signaling from hill tops. The lightweight flags were at times make in a square, versus usual rectangular shape to conserve the valuable fabric. In a more unique utilization, silk was used for observation balloons during the Civil War by both sides. The most famous usage was by Professor Thaddeus Sobieski Constantine Lowe. Not a particularly educated man, he took the "Professor" title to emphasize his supposedly elevated (no pun intended) scientifically inspired showmanship.

Only one week after the firing on Fort Sumter, this colorful man hoped to fly the Atlantic in his beautiful balloon. A test flight was made in Cincinnati, Ohio. After nine hours drifting on the prevailing westerly air currents, he appeared descending near Unionville, South Carolina. In another irony of nomenclature, the citizens of Unionville were not at least predominantly Unionists. Lowe was initially suspected of spying. Fortunately for his future aeronautical efforts, a local man vouched for his nonmilitary role and he and his beloved balloon, Enterprise, were sent out of Confederate territory by train. This close call did not hinder Lowe from really joining the Union Army as a member of General George B. McClellan's staff. He had actually demonstrated a potential military usefulness as he had performed a flight over Washington, DC. There, on June 17th of 1861, President Lincoln received telegraph communication from Lowe and representatives of American Telegraph Company from 500 ft elevation.[167]

In order to begin a balloon observation program, seven balloons were procured by the U.S. military. These were to be tethered by 3 or 4 spools of 5,000 feet cables. Even though Lowe was officially a member of the military, the "Balloon Corps" was under the command of the Army's Chief Topographical Engineer.[168] Only a handful of men were enlisted for this service. Specially trained men were assigned to balloon support, "one man to varnish the envelopes, two generator assistants, one repairman, on machinist, and one permanent orderly." [169]

The lucky or potentially unlucky balloon pilots were most active in Virginia during the Peninsular Campaign and in military engagements in mid-Virginia, including at Gaines Mill, Seven Pines and at Hanover Courthouse. Flights were made both during the day, with messages conveyed to terra firma by weighted note sent down the tethers, by telegraph, by visual signals, at time transmitted from one balloon to another in a relay form. Nighttime communication was more vivid, through the use of "oxy-hydrogen searchlights with eight-inch reflectors", telegraph or flares. The night flights basically attempted to estimate the size and location of the enemy encampments by counting campfires.

The Confederates, logically, wanted their own balloons. Not wanting to miss out, Dr.

---

[166] History of Sericulture, Cultural Entomology Digest, by Dr. Ron Cherry, pg. 2
[167] http.//www.thaddeuslowe.name/CWPeninsula Campaign.htm pg 1
[168] http.//www.thaddeuslowe.name/CWPeninsula Campaign.htm pg 2
[169] Pg. 2

Edward Cheves of Savannah, Georgia, "bought all the silk in Savannah and Charleston, developed a varnish (made of old rubber railcar springs dissolved in oil) to make the silk airtight, and constructed a balloon."[170] General Robert E. Lee put this balloon under the command of Lieutenant Edward Porter Alexander in 1862. Fascinatingly, Alexander desired to operate a balloon department superior to the Union efforts. His personal struggle included, "a fear of heights that followed him from his days at West Point. This fear was overcome through counseling by Dr Cheves."[171] His destiny was manifest.

While the Confederate crew was working to be superior to the Union balloonists, the balloon was not. In comparison to the northern balloons, which could be inflated within 3 hours, incredibly stay afloat for up to 2 WEEKS, and were filled by mobile gas generators, the Confederate balloon was filled with "illuminating gas from the Richmond Gas Works" or by heated air generated by burning pinecones that had been saturated with turpentine. This silk balloon could only support the basket for a maximum of 7 hours and could only ascend to about 1,000 feet, which was an elevation easily exceeded by the Yankee observers. Only two Confederate balloons were constructed and both were captured by 1863. The Union had a total of seven military balloons already by the end of 1861. While the large, floating, slowly moving bags of gas were frequent targets for the ground based troops none were literally shot down. Some crashed, some were captured and the fad ended well before the end of the War. Likely, both the northern and southern balloonists came to the opinion that "Prussian General Helmuth Karl Bernhard von Moltke did in 1859, that the technical challenges posed by balloons outweighed their military potential"[172].

---

[170] http://www.thaddeuslowe.name/CWPeninsulaCampaign.htm pg 5
[171] Pg. 5
[172] Pg. 6

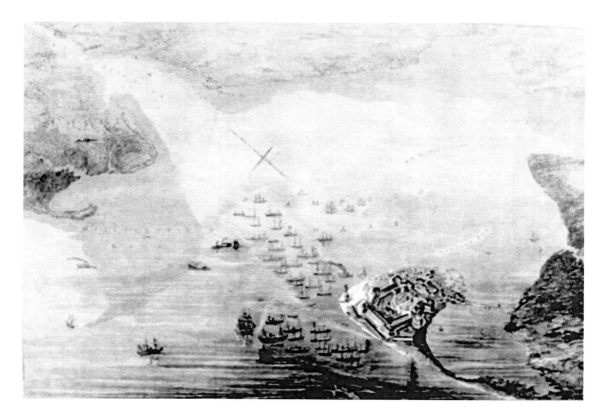

Figure 59 - Balloon View of Fortress Monroe and Hampton Roads

Harper's Pictorial History of Civil War, pg. 132

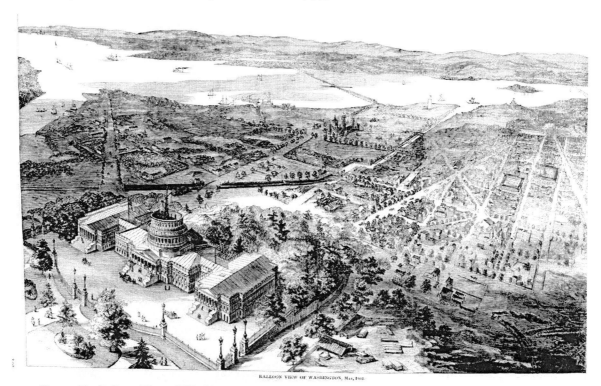

BALLOON VIEW OF WASHINGTON, May, 1861

Figure 60 - Balloon View of Washington, DC, May 1861

Harper's Pictorial History of the Civil War, vol. 1, 1866, pg. 134

DAVID D. PORTER.

Figure 61 - David D. Porter, The Creative Admiral

Harper's pg. 730

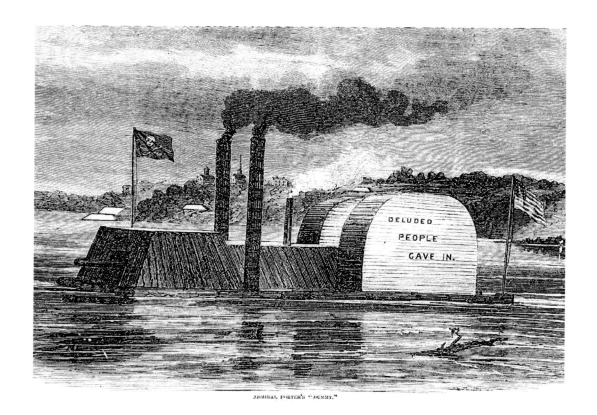

ADMIRAL PORTER'S "DUMMY."

Figure 62 - Admiral Porter's Dummy

Harper's pg. 432

Figure 63 - Creative Disguising of Union Masts. Did you see that tree move?

Leslie's pg. 274

PORTER'S MORTAR FLEET IN TRIM.

Figure 64 - Porter's Mortar Fleet in Trim , Vines and Boughs

Harper's pg. 439

Figure 65 - Federal Mortar Boats in Action on the Mississippi River

Leslie's pg. 117

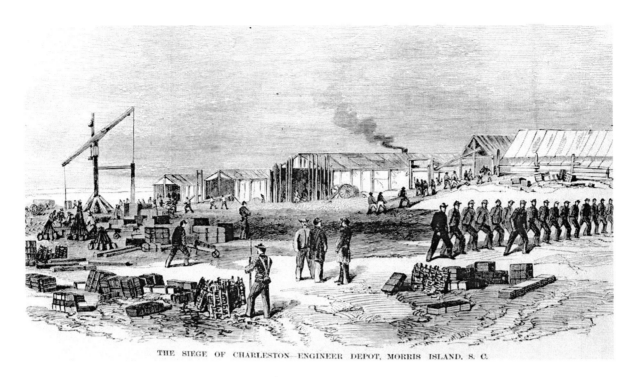

THE SIEGE OF CHARLESTON—ENGINEER DEPOT, MORRIS ISLAND, S. C.

Figure 66 - Engineer Depot at Morris Island

Leslie's pg. 474

Figure 67 - General Burnside Riding in High Style or What Your Railroad Can Do For You

Leslie's pg. 162

DESTROYING RAILROADS.

Figure 68 - Vital Railroad Destruction

Harper's 456

Figure 69 - Loss of Vital Southern Railroad During Sherman's March across Georgia

Leslie's pg. 447

Figure 70 - Rebuilding Railway by Union Troops after Burning of Bridge by Confederates

Leslie's pg. 211

Figure 71 - Railroad Supplies

Harper's pg. 521

Figure 72 - Destruction of Naval Yard and Ships at Norfolk to Prevent use by Confederates

Harper's pg. 82 and 83

Figure 73 - Destruction of Tybee Island Lighthouse by Confederates

Leslie's pg. 307

Figure 74 - Distributing Rations and Appointing a Knapsack Guard before a Reconnaissance mission

Leslie's pg. 343 "Our sketch represents the Federal soldiers receiving their rations and the appointment of a guard for their knapsacks. Thanks to our Illustration the exempts, whether sneaks, aliens, valetudinarians, or members of that peace society, the Home Guards, could get a pretty accurate idea of a soldier life, and be present in spirit with their noble brothers on whom they had devolved the sacred duty of battle."

Figure 75 - Richmond, VA view from Belle Isle prison camp in the James River.

Information below indicates that this about 1.5 acre island was the site "where on an average ten thousand Federal soldiers imprisoned and slowly tortured." Confederate capitol is in distance, rail bridge of the Richmond and Petersburg Railroad is to right. Interestingly, the huge Haxall Flouring Mill, stated to be the largest of its kind in the world, is the thirteen stories high building at the end of the bridge. This prison camp was no worse than others both North and South.

Leslie's pg. 430

Figure 76 - Union occupation in Brownsville, Texas. Captured King Cotton

Leslie's pg. 412

Figure 77 - A Sutler's Store, Harper's Ferry, VA-From a Sketch in 1862. Appears to be an

Leslie's History Pg. 209

CUTTING COARSE FORAGE INTO CHAFF.

Figure 78 - Foraging for Chaff

Leslie's pg 448

Figure 79 - Confederate Oats

Leslie's pg. 106

Chapter Sixteen - Not Everything is What It Appears to Be

As silk could not substitute for cotton, other basic commodities that were in short supply were forged. Census figures documented the differences between supply and demand in the southern states versus northern states. While industrialization is usually viewed to be productive of durable goods, such as wrought iron, textile weaving, paper printing, ship building and weapons manufacturing, Some creative products were much less durable or actually expendable. One such example, specifically to exhibit t to enemy observers such as those in silk balloons, were wooden cannons. This odd weapon was used by both the north and south prior to and during the Civil War. While most were dummy, nonfunctioning replicas of cannon, some actually were firing models. The most commonly seen artificial cannon were simply logs propped up to look like barrels. These were named "Quaker Guns," taking their name from pacifist members of the Religious Society of Friends, also known as Quakers.

Firing, severely atypical cannons were made. Cherry logs, or other hardwoods could be used for barrels. The legendary historian, Bruce Catton, included the picture of a wooden mortar in his account of the siege of Vicksburg in 1863. While very dangerous, firing a few shots of projectiles, wooden balls, iron balls or even rocks, with poor accuracy, was possible. This alternative reflected the fact that the south had limited availability to cannon s.

While the Union Army was more blessed with armament manufacturers, the northerners did resort to fakery as well. In an effort to draw Confederate fire and hasten the demise of southern guns, Union Admiral David Dickson Porter attempted to give the enemy something to shoot at and not risk his own valuable ships. While Porter struggled to gain control of the Mississippi in February 1863, he utilized iron clad gunboats to run the River below Confederate gun emplacements. One magnificent example of Union resources was the Indianola. This remarkable ship was one hundred and seventy-four feet long, with fifty foot beam, with "ten feet from the top of her deck to the bottom of her keel, or eight feet four inches in the clear."[173]

Over an oak hull, thirty-two inches thick, three inch thick plates of iron. The deck was eight inches thick oak with one inch overlying iron sheets. On the deck was a casement or gun house with walls constructed with an angle of 26 ½ degrees, with three inches covering of iron. All her engines were located below deck, with coal bunkers seven feet thick alongside her five steam generating boilers. Seven engines were on board, two for powering propellers, two for capstans, two for the side wheels that churned the dark Mississippi, and one for water pumping from the bilge, firefighting and supplying water for the crew. The guns were also state of the art. The casement was ported for two forward pointing guns in addition to one on each side, and four more guns to cover the sides and stern. Two of these forward weapons were 11 inch Dahlgren guns, and two others in the after casement were 9 inch guns. Also creativity was expended in

---

[173] Harper's Pictorial History of the Civil War, first edition, pg 450

the addition of hose that was capable of spraying scalding, boiling water the length of the ship.[174]

Unfortunately, this ship became the target of the Webb, a Confederate ram.. With 6 blows from this ramming vessel, the Indianola lost her starboard rudder, started taking on water too quickly for crew and bilge pumps to control. Outnumbered on this particular night the Indianola ran ashore and threw functioning guns overboard. Porter thought the Indianola was a good platform for her battery but recognized other weaknesses in the cumbersome vessel. He did note that she drew Confederate attention and fire. As the Indianola and other ships ran the River below Vicksburg, the Union Admiral noted that five enemy guns were burst and destroyed by repetitive firing at the gunboats. To draw more fire and self-destruction from the Confederate batteries, Porter constructed his naval version of Quaker guns. Taking "'An old coal-barge, picked up in the river, was the foundation to build on. It was built of old boards in twelve hours, with pork-barrels on top of each other for smoke-stacks, and two old canoes for quarter-boats; her furnaces were built of mud, and only intended to make black smoke and not steam..' Porter sent the "Dummy" out on the night of February 24th, 1863. It drew fire from Vicksburg Confederates by early morning light. It was also initially felt that this sham ship or "monster gun-boat" was chasing the Confederate ship the Queen of the West at a rate of about 4 miles per hour or about 5 knots. In hind sight, the ship appeared unsinkable as southern shells passed through the vessel and the speed of progress down river was the speed of the River current, itself. Union troops under General Ulysses S. Grant laughed.[175]

---

[174] Harper's pg 450
[175] Harper's pg 451

Figure 80 - Army Scenes Pontoon Bridge

Harper's pg. 350

Figure 81 - Negroes at Work on Canal If you don't have a river, make one **Harper's pg. 45**

While the Unionists enjoyed the farce, Confederates busied themselves with reclaiming cast off weapons, scuttled guns and ships, clothing, medicines and any other essential products which fell into their hands. Recycling efforts were impressive and much more urgent for the southern states. The very issue of ship building was another microcosm of the southern industrialization compared to the North. Probably the most famous of these recycled ships was the Merrimac, rechristened as the CSS Virginia. This iron clad held its own in Hampton Roads versus the Union, cheese box on a raft design iron clad known in history as the Monitor.

Likewise many of the most effective small arms of the Confederacy were procured from the north. Almost one-third of smoothbore muskets in the south at the onset of war came from confiscated Union stores. Most of these were percussion-cap utilizing muskets of Model 1842. Some older and less efficient Model 1822 muskets were still in use but generally refitted with percussion caps rather than notoriously inefficient flint. Much more accurate and prevalent during the Civil War were muzzle-loading shoulder arms with rifled barrels. Fifty thousand such guns were in U.S. arsenals in 1861. Most were .54 caliber originally, but thousands were re-bored to .58 caliber. In the northern states the most commonly manufactured rifled musket was the Massachusetts made Springfield. Incredibly, Springfield alone increased annual manufacturing of rifles from 20,000 to 200,000 during the Civil War. Not surprisingly the most commonly used rifled barrel muzzle loader in the Confederacy was the Enfield, made in England. This model with a .577 bore could fire the minie ball designed for the .58 caliber Springfield. As arsenals or supply depots or even battlefield casualties could be raided by southern troops the weapons and ammunition were placed in service for the enemy quickly. Over the course of the War, the Confederacy purchased about 580,000 rifles overseas.[176]

Similarly, the most desirable of shoulder firing weapons, the breech-loading carbine, was attainable to the average Confederate only through capture or at extremely high prices from blockade runners. While a very proficient soldier could load and fire approximately 3 shots in a minute, the copper cartridge, breech loading Sharps carbine could fire ten rounds in one minute. Due to this impressive fire power, a similar breech-loader, the Spencer carbine, became very popular with the Union cavalry. With a magazine holding seven copper rim fire .52 caliber waterproof cartridges, it was said by outmanned and under-armed Confederates that this weapon could, "load up on Sunday and shoot all the rest of the week."[177] Interestingly, the inventor of the Spencer carbine, C. M. Spencer, actually sold the U.S. Navy on his gun by loading his carbine, burying it, soaking it in salt water and then firing it 250 times without cleaning it,. He also demonstrated a firing rate of 21 shots per minute.[178] Even if the gun itself fell into the hands of a Southerner, the ammunition often did not. With the paucity of copper and bronze smelting the South was in no position to keep up with the Union in arms and ammunition manufacturing. In addition, the wealthier, non-blockaded North purchased 726,000 small arms from Europe by August of 1862, while the very limited Confederacy obtained only 50,000 similar weapons from overseas.

---

[176] http://en.wikipedia.org/wiki/Rifles_in_the_American_Civil_War#cite_note-keegan2009-0
[177] History Buff's Guide to the Civil War, by Thomas R. Flagel, pg. 105
[178] Carbines, Revolving Rifles, and Repeating Rifles, by Robert Neipurt
http://www.floridareenactorsonline.com/carbinesetc.htm

RECEPTION OF WOUNDED SOLDIERS BY THE FEDERAL AUTHORITIES AT FORTRESS MONROE, VA.—THE CARS CONVEYING THEM TO THE HOSPITAL—SURGEONS DRESSING THEIR WOUNDS

Figure 82 - Microcosm of the Union war effort. Steam paddlewheels, silk flags, crated supplies, black laborers, the injured and dying soldiers, primitive nurses in dresses and hats of the era

Leslie's pg. 158

THE WINANS GUN.

Figure 83 - Winan Steam Driven Gun—Unsuccessful Attempt at Southern Ingenuity

Harper's pg. 103

In antebellum years, copper mines and smelters were located in Tennessee, but were owned by Northern based companies which closed the operations with the onset of War in late 1861. When these were captured by the Confederate troops in 1863, they were sold to Southerners and reopened on a smaller scale to attempt to obtain this essential metal. Unfortunately, these sites were recaptured by the Union in 1863. No creativity could replace this commodity. [179]

Similarly to the predicament of small arms shortages in the South, large guns were also in short supply. In addition to the capture of Federal arsenals and personal weapons, the Confederacy took control of U.S. coastal defense large siege guns but very few mobile, field artillery pieces. Most of these were smooth bore cannons lacking the range and accuracy of breech loading cannon with rifled barrels. The only manufacturer of cannon in the South at the start of the hostilities was the Tredegar factory in Richmond.

At the onset of War, neither side possessed rifled field weapons, however the Union could soon manufacture both bronze and iron models. The South was limited in great degree to iron guns due to the shortage of bronze, an alloy of tin and copper Again, not everything produced during the War was what it seems. On a basic level, siege guns were mounted large artillery found in coastal forts, siege or garrison artillery which were transportable to siege lines, smaller mountain artillery which were even lighter and transportable by horses or mules, and the even lighter field artillery. These weapons were defined by the weight of their projectiles, as "pounders." The barrel types were further defined as older, less accurate smoothbore, or as more recently manufactured, more accurate, rifled barreled models. In addition these larger artillery pieces were further described as "guns" or "howitzers."[180]

Guns generally have longer barrels, fired solid shot, over a low trajectory, with larger loads or pounds of gunpowder Howitzers, on the other hand, were shorter barreled pieces, firing exploding shells or shots over higher trajectories, using lighter weight gunpowder loads, were much more mobile, usually smoothbore artillery pieces.

While the U.S. government had about 4,000 artillery pieces at the onset of War, only about 165 were vital field artillery pieces. The North quickly made up for antiquated artillery through creative and very productive foundries such as West Point Foundry in Cold Spring, New York. There, former U.S. Army Captain Robert P. Parrett developed a reinforced cast iron, rifled gun. While older smoothbore models required less strength due to looser fitting projectiles, cast iron barrels were prone to bursting when under the much greater pressure from tight fitting projectiles coming into contact with rifling grooves. Parrott developed his Parrott Rifle by enforcing the most vulnerable breech area with a shrink fitted band of cast iron around the iron barrel. His process included a slow rotation of the barrel as this heated band cooled. This helped get a more complete, even seal between the band and barrel than that achieved from gravity pulling down during cooling on a stationary barrel. Likewise, the Rodman technique addressed this effort to strengthen the barrel by piping water into the bore of the barrel where the metal would cool more evenly. Even with these methods, artillery crews were subject to erratic

---

[179] http://www.telliquah.com/History2.htm
[180] http://www.civilwarartillery.com/basicfacts.htm pg. 3

bursting of barrels on a size guns and howitzers.

Interestingly, one of the earliest Parrott Rifles was bought by the Commonwealth of Virginia in 1860. Delivered to the Virginia Military Institute, this weapon was tested by the artillery professor, Thomas J. Jackson. Twelve more were ordered by Virginia from the West Point Foundry to help upgrade the State defenses (or offences, depending on perspective) . Unfortunately, the cast iron Parrott Rifles still tended to burst unpredictably, just beyond the reinforced breech area. Approximately 500-600 were made in the North, while only about 150 were made in the South from Union specifications.

While Stonewall Jackson approved of the Parrott, E. Porter Alexander, as artillery commander under Confederate General James Longstreet favored the Model 1841-24 pound Howitzer. In contrast, Union General George McClellan, Captain Henry Hunt, future Chief of Artillery for the Union's Army of the Potomac, and Confederate commander Robert E. Lee favored the famed Model 1857 Light 12-pound gun. This weapon only resembled a howitzer in that it could fire a shell, as projectile. In popular vernacular this versatile gun was known as the, "Napoleon," after the French leader who desired a standardized, versatile, cost effective artillery piece. Lee even, "suggested that all 6-pdrs be melted down and recast into Napoleons."[181]

The south did little recasting, but more re-boring calibers to use other more prevalent sizes of ammunition and actually rifling old smooth bore pieces. The North did use bronze for many smooth bore artillery pieces but the relatively soft alloy did not hold up well in rifled barrels. The South did not have the iron supply of the North, but even more so lacked the resources to make much bronze. The cast iron barrels were 5-6 times less expensive than those of bronze.[182] To overcome the critical brittleness of iron and the softness of bronze, a very creative man, John Griffen, developed a stronger barrel made by, "welding together bundles of wrought iron rods then passing the whole through a rolling mill."[183] This Model 1861 3-inch Ordnance Rifle was lighter in weight, very transportable, and regarded as the best of Civil War muzzle loading artillery pieces. While about 1000 were made in the North, none were manufactured in the South. Due to general shortages Union batteries were generally composed of 4 guns and 2 howitzers. Confederate batteries were more commonly made of 4 guns. With a well-trained gun crew, two rounds per minute could be fired. This differential magnified the manpower issues. Unfortunately, while a usual ratio of 2-4 artillery pieces were in place per 1,000 soldiers, the Confederacy at times reached a ratio of 8-10 pieces per 1,000 men, reflecting the manpower shortages rather than a bounty of artillery. Likewise, significant differences were evident in supplies. In the battle of Gettysburg, each Union gun averaged a total of 270 rounds of ammunition, while the Confederates averaged about 230 rounds per gun.[184]

This disparity was again foreseeable from the Census efforts. Between manpower deficits, manufacturing shortages, natural resources shortages, transportation deficiencies and importation blockade, the Confederate Army fought a losing War for a surprising 4 years. All wars are wars of attrition.

---

[181] http://www.civilwarhome.com/artillery.htm pg 3
[182] Pg .6
[183] Pg. 6
[184] Battle In the Civil War, Generalship and Tactics in America 1861-1865, Paddy Griffith, pg. 26

Figure 84 - Colored Infantry Bringing in Captured Guns Amid Cheers at the Siege of Petersburg, VA

Leslie's pg. 438

Figure 85 - The Twenty-second Colored Regiment, Duncan's Brigade, Union troops, a relatively untapped Southern resource Leslie's pg. 438

Figure 86 - Signal Flag

Harper's pg. 396

RACTICING WITH THE CELEBRATED SAWYER GUN ON THE CONFEDERATE BATTERIES AT SEWELL'S POINT, NEAR NORFOLK, FROM FORT CALHOUN, ON THE RIPRAPS, IN FRONT OF FORTRESS MONROE.

Figure 87 - Sawyer Gun with Signal Flag Leslie's pg. 250

SIGNALING WITH A PIECE OF LOOKING GLASS.

Figure 88 - Not a great communication system on a cloudy day or at night. Leslies' pg. 448

Figure 89 - Signal Station. Not for those with a fear of heights or much common sense

Leslie's pg. 396

Chapter Seventeen - Hungry for Success

The decade between 1850 and 1860 was one of the most pivotal in U.S. history. Immigration, inventions, natural resources, and westward expansion, set the stage for incredible opportunities for legal and illegal profiteering. Speculators arose in industry, imports, exports, and agriculture. Northerners and Southerners were greedy and unencumbered by modern versions of income tax. Gold was the gold standard and the most recent internal migration was into California by the "miners, forty-niners," with or without their daughter, Clementine. These miners, immigrants, planters and industrialists all felt a hunger, either monetarily or gastric, or both. As history books often stress the mechanical developments, agriculture also advanced. The census reflected the ability of the expansive population of the cities to be fed by a relatively smaller segment of the population. In addition, massive quantities of grains were exported.

In the "Leading Articles Produced in the Western States, which included Kentucky" as delineated in the records of "Manufactures of the West," "Flour and Meal" was the most valuable of commodities. The value of this category in just this area of the United States in 1850 totaled over $42 ½ million dollars. In 1860 this value exceeded $96 million. These amounts also far exceeded the second place produce of value, "Lumber, sawed and planed," by $28 million dollars in 1850 and over $63 million in 1860. Most of the grain was used in bread and cracker manufacturing, but sizable quantities of rye, barley, and hops went into alcohol or liquor production. The U.S. used over 11 million bushels of corn, 3.7 million bushels of barley, 2.1 million bushels of rye, and 1.2 tons of hops in 1860. The overwhelming majority was used in the Northern states. The state of New York used over 2 million bushels of barley by itself. Ohio, alone, used almost 3.6 million bushels of corn.[185] While other profiteering industries could more easily hold back different types of durable goods, farmers had the ultimate nondurable products.

Food production fell as the Civil War wore on. Even though the South was agrarian and slave labor centered, the agricultural focus was profit driven in cotton, tobacco and sugar cane production. With labor shortages, rickety rail system, extremely and increasingly devalued currency, and armies marching across agricultural lands, the Confederacy experienced true hunger pains. The central government of the states' rights stressing South tried to legislate and force the planters to shift to edible staple crops. Even where early forms of Victory Gardens were planted and produced, the crops were difficult to harvest and transport to the needy. Restless, hungry southerners protested with bread riots in the winter of 1862 and in April 1863.

The most famous riot based on public hunger occurred on April 2, 1863 in Richmond, Virginia. In a display of personal concern, bordering on desperation, President Jefferson Davis mounted a wagon, emptied his pocket of change and threw it to the angry, vociferous crowd. He managed to disperse the largely female crowd after threatening that he would give the order for

---

[185] Eighth Census, pg. 159

the Virginia Militia to fire at them. This episode reflects the fact that cities were particularly susceptible to mass hunger due to the concentration of population, relative to the location of food producing farms. Gardens were encouraged but the food supply had to be enhanced with importation from other sources. Since the limited railroad system was overwhelmed, with the blockade limiting import from overseas, the north and from across the Mississippi River, the internal rivers and canals of the Confederacy were used for movement of crops and produce into cities.

A system of bartering attempted to avoid the use of devalued Confederate paper currency. With a larger proportion of the population absent for military service, those remaining had to meet more of their own needs as well as those of neighbors and fellow countrymen. Examples of the use of available labor for food production were seen in the hospital systems of the South and North. With the large concentrations of needy, hungry, ill or wounded soldiers, many hospitals were supplied with produce from their own gardens. Bakeries were also commonly on site and at least at times produced excess loaves which were sold or traded to the civilian population for necessary supplies. The two largest Confederate Hospitals near Richmond, Chimborazo and Winder, each had huge bakeries with convalescent patients helping produce their daily bread. Chimborazo's bakery produced up to 10,000 loaves per day for the patients and staff. Vegetables, meat and milk were supplied from a nearby farm, "Tree Hill." This hospital enterprise was overseen by one of the South's most capable young physicians, Dr. James B. McCaw. In nearly 100 wooden buildings, with a staff of 20-30 physicians, hired slaves and with the lesser ill patients taking care of the more severely ill, up to 4,000 patients per day were cared for.[186]

Even though 5 railways converged at Richmond, canal boats were important to the food chain. One such boat, *The Chimborazo,* transported cotton yarn from "Tree Hill" up the James River to western Virginia, in the area of Lynchburg and Lexington, to barter for food.[187]

In a very creative recycling effort, "the grease from its five great soup kitchens was mixed with lye that had been brought through the blockade to make soap."[188]

Fortunately for the Union, the westward expansion into very rich, arable lands, with expanding transportation access and distance from battlefield sites, food supplies were generally more adequate in the North. Inflation did affect the purchasing power of the Union military and civilians. Prices soared and the rich got richer, the poor got poorer. Certain commodities were particularly in demand. The Union soldiers wanted Confederate tobacco, and sugar cane, and the Southern troops wanted almost everything from the Northerners. Some of these products were bartered across lines by the typical Johnny Reb and Billy Yank. Other more personal items were pilfered from the dead. More specialized essential materials such as medical supplies and medications were expensive items procured by blockade runners or black market or illegal trade over battle-lines.

---

[186] http://www.nps.gov/rich/historyculture/chimborazo.htm
[187] Images of Civil War Medicine, Gordon Dammann, DDS and Alfred Jay Bollet, MD ,pg 150
[188] Images, pg. 150

Figure 90 - Communication by Courier or looking for tobacco for pipe

Harper's 538

MAJOR ANDERSON'S CANDLESTICK.

Figure 91 - Creative Candleholder Harper's pg. 27

Figure 92 – Army Scenes –It is Interesting to note that drinking around bucket in lower right center is followed by grave in right lower corner. Frequently true. Harper's pg. 350

Figure 93 - Grocer on the River **Leslie's pg. 32**

Attempts were made to grow poppies for opium and morphine production in the South but these were unsuccessful. Other creative efforts were made to supply milk, meat, tea, and coffee.

The North was blessed with a supply of a new form of milk that could travel with the soldiers outside of the natural canteen, a cow's udder. In 1856, Gail Borden developed sweetened condensed milk. This innovator is regarded as "father of the modern dairy industry." Through initial experimentation Borden was financially broke by 1855 but found funding through Jeremiah Milbank. (another individual with a fitting surname) Together with the brain and the financial brawn, Borden founded the New York Condensed Milk Company in southeastern New York state.

He capitalized, literally, on the fragility of milk and on the resources of his area. Borden realized that cow's milk is about 87% water. Bulk and spoilage were major dairy enemies. Milk was transported in the early 1850s in oak barrels with were less than sanitary. He reasoned that the water content could be boiled off at low heat, leaving a milk concentrate. If this process would be carried out in vacuum sealed vats or pans, it should be much more stable and relatively free of spoilage. [189]

Borden's plant took advantage of his location in Putnam County, New York and ready rail access into New York City, to sell his product to the burgeoning population. The Civil War hastened the Company's growth and a factory was built in Brewster, New York in 1864. This plant location was quite ideal, in that it was on the Croton River to supply waterpower, in a dairy farming area, and also with rail access to national markets. In a brilliant, patriotic gesture,

---

[189] http://www.southeastmuseum.org/html/borden_s_milk.html

the factory produced, Eagle Brand Consolidated Milk. With rapid growth, the factory obtained milk from over 200 farms and employed approximately 100 men and women.[190] In the War, this product was not legally in the Confederacy. Very limited supply most likely entered the South through black market trade or through captured Union supplies. This milk had been sweetened with sugar, originally thought to act as a preservative and was commonly known as sweetened condensed milk. Union soldiers enjoyed this milk with their hardtack as "milk toast."[191]

One common use was as an additive to coffee. Southerners had little access to milk or cream or, for that matter, even coffee of a traditional type. With blockade, inflation, poor transportation, and massive demand unreached by supply, coffee became one of the most valuable commodities in the South. Since 1832, when President Andrew Jackson included coffee and sugar in the standard military rations, soldiers of both sides expected their java. The Union quartermasters attempted to supply high quality coffee beans, either green which would be roasted in the field, or in an already pre-roasted brown from. The standard military

SCENE IN CAMP LIFE CHIMNEY ARCHITECTURE THE FEDERAL SOLDIERS AT THEIR CAMP FIRES

Figure 94 - Creative Chimney Architecture

Harper's

ration was ten pounds of green or eight pounds of roasted coffee per 100 troops. In order to grind coffee beans in camp settings, every 100 soldiers were to be dispensed one rifle with a coffee grinder built into the stock. The Confederates' ration was to be the same amount of coffee but this goal was not attainable.

---

[190] http://www.southeastmuseum.org/html/borden_s_milk.html
[191] http://www.murfreesboropost.com/news.php?viewStory=1313, Mike West

Some very fortunate Confederate pickets or front line men could contact Union front men and barter tobacco for coffee. Across the Confederacy, coffee substitutes were essential for the mass population, military and nonmilitary. An amazing variety of substances were tried in order to replicate the original article. Chicory was the most widely accepted and preferred substitute. Other also ran organics were, beets, turnips, sweet potatoes, bread crusts, okra, rye, barley, peanuts, bran, chestnuts, cow-peas, persimmons, rice, beans, watermelon seeds, sorghum,

Figure 95 - Feeding the Poor At New Orleans

Harper's Pictorial, pg. 277

yams, carrots, corn meal, (my personal favorite) ASPARAGUS, parsnips, wheat, field peas, red wheat, sassafras nuts, beech root, horse beans, corn grits, dandelion, sugar cane seed, molasses and acorns. It is quite certain that resourceful individuals tried even other coffee substitutes. It is also plausible that some of these are not recorded in the written histories since the ingestion may have been fatal or at least embarrassingly not palatable. Most of these were recommended as coffee additives, to stretch or to extend the coffee made from coffee beans, usually Arabica. By 1862, the Union distributed an "essence of coffee" in which a concentrate of premixed coffee, milk and sugar was shipped in ½ gallon tins to be mixed as one teaspoon to one cup of hot water.[192] This was apparently not successful and was soon terminated.

Two of these extenders disserve special mention. Acorns were particularly of use, bountiful

---

[192] http://www.cfcwrt.com/thismonth9.html (the Cape Fear Civil War Round Table, That Indispensable Civil War Coffee! By Ann Hertzler pg. 1

throughout the South, and apparently palatable. Of the different types of oaks, acorns of White Oaks, Quercus Alba, were most tasty. The harvested acorns had, "The hard outer shell is removed, and the kernel is preserved, which, after being roasted, is ground with ordinary coffee."[193]

In the history of France, acorns were also used for subsistence during the famine of 1709. At that time, the acorns were ground into flour and used for bread. Black oak, red oak and other varieties of Quercus made stronger and "more astringent" coffee.[194]

It was commonly felt that these extenders saved the people of the Confederacy huge sums of money. According to the Little Rock Arkansas True Democrat of January 30, 1862, "In 1860, the importation of coffee in the then United States was the enormous amount of two hundred millions of pounds, at a cost of fifteen millions of dollars. The people of the South use doubly as much coffee as the people of the North. Nearly one-half of this vast sum was expended by the people of the Confederacy. If a substitute could be found, it would save us seven millions of dollars a year.."[195] The Southern reserve of coffee was used up and few could afford the skyrocketing drink. The price per pound in 1861 was $3.00, in 1862 was up to $4.00 per pound, in 1863 was up to $30.00 and by 1864 was up to $60.00 per pound in the Confederacy.[196] Real coffee was a true luxury.

Figure 96 - Distributing Rations and Appointing a Knapsack Guard before a reconnaissance mission

Leslie's pg. 343 "Our sketch represents the Federal soldiers receiving their rations and the appointment of a guard for their knapsacks. Thanks to our Illustration the exempts, whether sneaks, aliens, valetudinarians, or members of that peace society, the Home Guards, could get a

---

[193] http:ww.uttyler.edu/vbetts/coffee.htm pg 6
[194] Pg. 9
[195] Pg. 10
[196] http://www.cfcwrt.com/thismonth9.html (the Cape Fear Civil War Round Table, That Indispensable Civil War Coffee! By Ann Hertzler pg. 1

pretty accurate idea of a soldier life, and be present in spirit with their noble brothers on whom they had devolved the sacred duty of battle."

Probably the most descriptive and creative of recipes for "the Times.—To make coffee.—Take tan bark, three parts; three old cigar stumps and a quart of water, mix well, and boil fifteen minutes in a dirty coffee pot, and the best judges cannot tell it from the finest Mocha."[197]

Unfortunately, acorn coffee and most of the substitutes did not have the caffeine jolt of real coffee. Interestingly, the cigar butts would likely impart some nicotine, which acts similarly to caffeine as a stimulant.

For those wishing to replace coffee with tea, this commodity was likewise in extremely short, and expensive supply. Substitutes also were advertised. Some of these were yopon (sic), rosemary, sassafras, sage, and strawberry leaves, but the best was generally felt to be made from meadow hay.

THE GREAT BAKERY FOR THE UNITED STATES ARMY AT THE CAPITOL, WASHINGTON, D. C.

Figure 97 - The Great Bakery for the United States Army at the Capitol, Washington, D.C.

Leslie's History pg. 167

---

[197] http://www.uttyler.edu/vbetts/coffee.htm pg. 5

BREAD-OVENS UNDER THE CAPITOL.

Figure 98 - Bread oven Under Capitol, Washington, D.C. Harper's pg. 109

ARMY COOKHOUSE CONSTRUCTED IN AN OLD CHIMNEY OF AN OUTHOUSE OF
THE LACY MANSION, ON THE RAPPAHANNOCK, FALMOUTH, VA.

Figure 99 - Creative Cookhouse from Recycled Chimney Leslie's 454

153

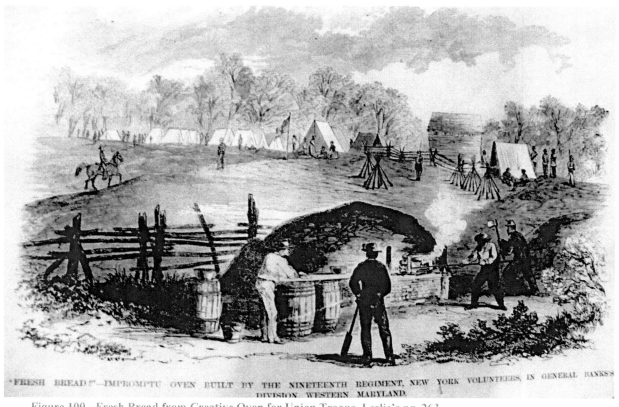

"FRESH BREAD!"—IMPROMPTU OVEN BUILT BY THE NINETEENTH REGIMENT, NEW YORK VOLUNTEERS, IN GENERAL BANKS'S DIVISION WESTERN MARYLAND.

Figure 100 - Fresh Bread from Creative Oven for Union Troops Leslie's pg. 263

SKETCHES OF ARMY LIFE—WEIGHING OUT RATIONS

Figure 101 - Sketches of Army Life—Weighing out Rations

The yopon (sic) was descriptively described in the Charleston Mercury of January 24, 1862 as, "the old woman's yopon (sic), that 'kept her out of heaven twenty years, bless God.'"[198] This yopon was correctly spelled "youpon," or "yaupon." This was technically "Ilex vomitoria." Unfortunately, the citizens of the South generally did not know the scientific nomenclature or they would have avoided this substance that included the term vomitoria, as in vomit, as in emesis. It is an "evergreen holly of the southeast United States, having lustrous red or sometimes yellow fruit, whose dried leaves are used to make a bitter tea. Also called cassina."[199] It is not surprising that so many died of diarrhea, dehydration, dysentery, and from water, (or tea, or coffee) borne pathogens. The only positive element of these heated beverages was that some pathogens were killed or at least attenuated over a camp fire or on a stove. Most recipes did not recommend out right boiling of the water, or preferred more gently steeping the substitutes in hot water. Even though basic knowledge of bacteriology and pathogenesis of infectious disease were some decades away, the United States Sanitary Commission supported the use of hot drinks to lessen the risk of diarrhea. Florence Nightingale, most legendary of nurses, wrote, "Directions for Camp and Hospital Cooking," in 1861. This manual was used by both the North and South, although shortages prevented ideal implementation. Alcohol would, of course, work better to prevent water borne diseases. Ironically, Andrew Jackson, Old Hickory, had replaced the traditional British military allotment of rum with coffee.[200]

Figure 102 - Sherman's —Dummers" Foraging in South Carolina

Leslie's pg. 432

---

[198] Pg. 10
[199] http://www.thefreedictionary.com/Yaupon
[200] http://www.murfreesboropost.com/news.php?viewStory=1313, pg 1 Did real coffee win the Civil War by Mike West

The quantity of coffee actually required for the soldiers was astronomical. Based on census returns from 1850, the antebellum United States army was a paltry 10,546 men, a third of which were native born. Another 7,500 men were in the U.S. navy with 82% being native born. In the 1860 Census, military returns were reported by the Office of the Adjutant General of the Army, to be an aggregate of 2 million men. As the South geared up for secession, 100,000 southerners volunteered for service in 1860, so many so that 1/3rd was sent home at this premature time.

By the time of mustering out of service on 6/1/65, more than one million men were in the military.

Initially, many were three month volunteers which were rapidly expanded to three year terms as both sides realized that the conflict was not to be short lived. Of these, the U.S. total of deaths in battle was 67,058, with those dying of wounds totaling 43,012, and another 40,154

BIVOUAC OF THE ELEVENTH INDIANA VOLUNTEER REGIMENT (ZOUAVES), COLONEL LEWIS WALLACE COMMANDING, AT CUMBERLAND, MD.

rtist who accompanied General McClellan's command sketched the gallant Eleventh Indiana Zouaves in their bivouac at Cumberland, Md. Great interest was attached to this regiment after its brilli

Figure 103 - Bivouac of the Eleventh Indiana Volunteer Regiment (Zouves), Colonel Lewis Wallace Commanding, at Cumberland, MD

Leslie's History p. 127

(Note the coffee pot. which was standard for both Union and Confederate units in bivouac. Note also the commander who is most famous for writing *Ben Hur, A Tale of the Christ*, which was published in 1880 after 7 years of research. He did "look back on Ben Hur as my best performance." This was significant as Lew Wallace did become a Union General and later served as Governor of the New Mexico Territory.)[201]

---

[201] http://www.ben-hur.com/benhur.html

dying of miscellaneous causes such as murder, accidents, or suicide. The most impressive cause of death was from disease, including the water borne diarrhea. This morbid category totaled 199,720 men. This was just the total for Union troops. Unfortunately, Confederate records for these losses are incomplete and combined deaths from these causes total at least 133,821.

In addition to the terminal illnesses, many men were driven to desert in order to escape for their own sake or for their families' benefit. In this enumeration, it is reported that 199,105 Union troops and 104,428 Confederate soldiers deserted. In addition, 212,608 U.S. troops were captured, with 16,431 paroled on the field. In comparison, 476,169 Confederates were captured, 248,599 of which were paroled on the field. Ironically, the totals reported for deaths in prison varied only by 4 men. The Union prison camps were claimed to be the site of demise for 30,152 Confederates. The Confederate camps, such as infamous Andersonville, were death camps for 30,156 Union soldiers.[202]

As foreseen by General Robert E. Lee, himself, "I can anticipate no greater calamity for the Country than dissolution. I am willing to sacrifice everything but Honor for preservation of Union. It would be accumulation of all evils we complain of." On 4/18/61, Lee met with President Lincoln at Blair House. On 4/20/61, Lee resigned and the next day was offered the leadership of the Confederate army. His skill as a general became legendary. All manner of "evils" also became legendary.[203]

HOW THE DAUGHTERS OF MARYLAND RECEIVED THE SONS OF THE NORTH AS THEY MARCHED AGAINST THE CONFEDERATE INVADERS—SCENE ON THE MARCH.

Figure 104 - Daughters of Maryland receiving Sons of the North—how safe is that bucket? Leslie's pg. 458

---

[202] Frank Leslies' Illustrated History of the Civil War, 1st edition 1895 pg
[203] Leslies pg.

WATER SKIN AND MODE OF CARRYING.

Figure 105 - Unsanitary Water Storage

Leslies pg. 448

SCENE IN CAMP LIFE—COMPANY MESS OF THE THIRTEENTH ILLINOIS VOLUNTEERS IN THEIR CAMP BEFORE CORINTH, MISS.

Figure 106 - Company Mess - - Appropriate title **Leslie's pg. 202**

Figure 107 - Return of freed Union Prisoners onboard "Louisiana" Coffee, Tea, or safer Alcohol Leslie's pg. 74

Figure 108 - Arrival and Departure of Federal Troops in Philadelphia, PA Safe beverages?

Leslie's pg. 77

Figure 109 - Exodus of Confederates from Atlanta; unsanitary food supplies

Harper's 619

COOKING IN CAMP—THE KITCHEN OF THE FREMONT DRAGOONS AT TIPTON, MO.

Figure 110 - Cooking in Camp Safe?

Leslie's pg. 139

Figure 111 - Campaign in the Mud. Do not lose the coffee pot on the pole!

Harper's pg. 419

CAMP ZAGONYI—ENCAMPMENT OF FREMONT'S ARMY ON THE PRAIRIE NEAR WHEATLAND, MO., OCTOBER 18TH, 1861

Figure 112 - Camp Life on the Prairie——coffee time

Leslie's pg. 244

Chapter Eighteen - Migration of Riches

Generally, the antebellum years were a time of expansion. The United States grew in land mass, population and wealth. Not inconsequentially, the rich got richer. Manifest destiny was expressed in the overview of the 1860 census, "The form of our government, so attractive on account of the promise held out to all of participation in its direction, and which guarantees perfect freedom of opinion on matters political and religious, in times past proved a powerful incentive, and doubtless continues, to some extent, to influence migration to our shores."[204] How encouraging for the human chattel still held in the southern states. Even more ironically, and modestly, this volume largely disregarded the hurricane of Civil War looming over the Mason-Dixon Line. While basically 13 states, similar to the original 13 colonies, claimed sovereignty of states over the centralized ruling government, the U.S. Congress was presented with this rosy, narcissistic statement: "Formerly, when the policy of some populous European states was controlled by feelings of religious bigotry and political restriction, the incentives to migrate were sufficient to bring to this country a class of persons distinguished for high moral excellence and enlightened political opinion, and the prosperity of our country may, in a great measure, be traced to the character of the early settlers, who were, providentially, impelled to seek here a refuge from the persecutions of religious bigotry and political exclusion at home. Whether now, when the spirit of toleration has become so liberal in most of the countries of Europe, we gain much, except numerically, by the increase from the latter cause, is perhaps problematical. As a general rule, they who select our country because of the certainty which it holds out for the most valuable acquisitions to our numbers, while such as can find no country in Europe sufficiently liberal for their opinions are apt to experience the moral restraints of our people to be so irreconcilable with their views, as to render them either uncomfortable in their obedience, or actively restless to remove the barriers to greater license."[205]

While enumerating the slave population in later pages, it was felt, "The great increase of the population of our country is due to the fact that here, more than anywhere else, every man may find occupation according to his talents, and enjoy resources according to his industry. Employment is open and inviting in commerce, manufactures, and the arts, and as these flourish, agriculture is promoted and made remunerative and profitable."[206] In likely the most ironic or ironies, the United States of 1860 was stated to have, "proof against those sudden revolutions so destructive to the morals, industry, and economy of a nation."[207] It can be agreed upon that the Civil War was not "sudden," but was a revolution.

---

[204] U.S. Census, Introduction 1860, pg xxv
[205] U.S. Census 1860, pg xxvi
[206] Pg. xxvi
[207] Pg. xxvi

Figure 113 - Robert E. Lee

Leslie's pg. 80

Figure 114 - Confederate President Jefferson Davis

Leslie's pg 81

In the exuberant language of the antebellum years, immigration from Europe brought wealth as well as population increase. The North benefitted exponentially more than the South from this emigration. As a major increase in immigration began in 1847, the port of New York struggled to care for and process these new arrivals. A permanent commission was established to deal with this mixed blessing. The needs of these immigrants were astronomical. From 1847 to

1860, over 2 ½ MILLION aliens were cared for with "commutation and hospital money."[208]

Medical care for almost 200,000 individuals was supplied at the Marine Hospital and at the Emigrant's Refuge and Hospitals on Ward's Island. Over 300,000 were supplied with temporary room and board, and another 129,148 were provided with employment. "The total number of persons cared for, relieved, or forwarded, was 893,736, at an expense of $5,153,126."[209]

In the pre-Ellis Island era, the majority of United States immigrants entered the country at New York City. In 1855, an emigrant depot was opened named Castle Garden. For the next 16 months or so statistics were kept reflecting the tangible cash amounts entering the Country in the pockets of these immigrants. These records, as inaccurate as they may be, revealed approximately $68.00 claimed by each passenger arriving during this timeframe. First class passengers were felt to carry about $180.00 per person. This number was derived from Prussian statistics regarding the value immigrants carried out of the area.

These numbers translated into vast growth of the Northern economy as most immigrants stayed in the North. The majority of these passengers in 1860 arrived via ships from Liverpool, England. In this year alone, 1,149 ships came from Liverpool, 488 from Bremen, 386 from Havre, 303 from Hamburg, 296 from London, 150 from Antwerp, 86 from Glasgow and 70 from Rotterdam. Also reflecting the world's industrial progress, an increasing number of these ships were steam powered. In 1860, 373 sailing ship carried 74,435 passengers, as opposed to 109 steam powered vessels bringing a total of 34,247. It was reasoned that about 4 million emigrants entered the U.S. in 1860, with very few using the States as a stepping stone to ultimate emigration to Canada or even Mexico. Very significantly, an estimated $400,000,000.00 of personal wealth entered the country with these persons.[210] While acknowledging that many immigrants sent money to their homelands and relatives still there, the majority of this sum remained in the U.S. For instance, Great Britain began surveying banks and mercantile houses to see how much capital was sent back to England by their emigrants and found that between 1848 and 1860, over $56 millions of U.S. dollars were returned.

While census records do vary over the decennial frames in the size of the flow of immigrants, depending on wars, revolutions and job availability in homelands, arrival s in the U.S. felt the impact of Civil War. In 1859, 121,282 foreigners arrived, 153,640 in 1860, 91,919 in 1861 and 91,987 in 1862. These numbers are included rather oddly in the Census review of 1860 due to upgrading of additional information after the Census formally ended. The most remarkable single event to drive immigration to the U.S. was the famine in Ireland. The massive wave of "Exodus" from the Emerald Isle took place over eight years, beginning in 1847. At least 2,444,802 individuals emigrated. [211] Many of these people were poor, as, "It should also be observed, that besides the cash means, the immigrants in themselves represent physically, intellectually, and morally, a much greater capital."[212] The living conditions in the U.S. were generally improving over the years between the 7th and 8th Census. Despite the deplorable

---

[208] Pg. xxiii

[209] Pg. xxiii

[210] Census 1860, xxiv

[211] Census of 1860 ,pg xxiv

[212] Pg .xxiv

conditions of inner city tenements, the average number of occupants per dwelling decreased from 5.95 in 1850 to 5.5 in 1860. The highest average was in Rhode Island at 6.43 and southern states averaged about one full person less per dwelling. To keep this improvement in housing in perspective, Prussia averaged 7.52 per dwelling.

In the decade between 1850 and 1860, the eleven future Confederate States gained 88,256 persons, the future border- states, another 118,677 individuals, while the remaining states and territories gained 1,718,403 persons. It was further emphasized that 86.6% of the foreign-born U.S. population lived in free states and only 13.4% in slave-holding states. For every white immigrant that settled in the slave states, eight settled in free States.[213] This did not bode as well for Civil War victory for the South in 1860 as it did in 1850. In addition, four states, Alabama, Indiana, Louisiana and Mississippi became states of exodus or migration rather than states of immigration. All wars are wars of attrition. It also did not help the numbers in that the states of 1860 with greater than average mortality were those in the lowlands of the Atlantic coast and lower Mississippi River Valley.[214]

Over the same ten year period, white and free colored mortality, annual deaths, per cent, actually decreased. At the same time, slave mortality increased.[215] It was postulated that this may be somewhat inflated due to "a more full record by masters" or "may arise from increased labor during the season when cotton and sugar crops are gathered."[216] The age group with the most deaths, in all population groups (white, free colored, and slave) were those age 0-1 year.[217] On the other end of the life span were those over one hundred years of age. Several centenarians were recorded as dying in 1860. The oldest three listed were slaves. In a most suspicious, highly unlikely record, two died in Alabama at the age of 130 years and one died in Georgia at a Biblical sounding 137 years.

In 1860 Nineteen million Whites and less than 250,000 Blacks lived in the North; 8 millions of Whites and 4 million Blacks lived in the South. The number of white males of military age, 18-45 years, in the Southern states totaled 1,064,193 while the Northern states population of such men totaled 5,210,695. Another 413,370 such men lived in the border states of Kansas and Missouri. This means that the South had about 20% of potential military men compared to the North. For every 8 white immigrants locating in the free states, only one located to slave states. Of the decennial increase in foreign population immigrating to the U.S., with often industrial skills and manufacturing knowledge, the states with the greatest increase were New York, Illinois, Wisconsin, Pennsylvania, California, and Ohio. Those with least foreign increase were Vermont, Florida, North Carolina, South Carolina and Arkansas. Of these foreign born in 1850, the males outnumbered women 124 to 100, and in 1860 the ratio was 117 to 100. Most of these individuals also remained in the initial state to which they immigrated from overseas. Lastly the lowest mortality rate was seen in the "Alleghany region; the Northwestern States; the Pacific coast" while the highest mortality rates were present in the future Confederate areas, the lower Mississippi valley and lowlands of the Atlantic coast.[218] All wars are wars of attrition.

---

[213] Pg. xxx
[214] Pg .xlii
[215] Pg. xiv
[216] Pg .xlv
[217] Pg. xlv

THE ARMY OF GENERAL FREMONT ON ITS MARCH UP THE SHENANDOAH VALLEY—WOUNDED AND RAGGED SOLDIERS

Figure 115 - Ragged and Shoeless Soldiers Leslie's pg. 97

THE LAST SHOT.

Figure 116 - The Last Shot **Harper's pg. 771**

Chapter Nineteen - Northern Head, Southern Heart

By 1860, this differential was enumerated and all too evident if examined with a northern head instead of a southern heart. This ever increasing manufacturing strength of the Northern states was defined in the enumeration of heading number 7 of the 1860 census. Here any literate individual could read of the expanding, "*Kind of motive power, machinery, structure, or resource,*" in which the south was taking a back seat. This colorful terminology referred to the power sources, such as horses, water, wind, or water, and to the details of the physical plant used for manufacturing. These details could include numbers of printing presses, looms, saws, spindles, and the number of furnaces, ovens, fishing vessels, or bloomeries.[218] In the language of the time, "blooms" were transportable bars of iron that were smelted near the mines of origin and then transported to other manufacturing sites.[219] Further information was to be included in the number of employees, their wages and listing of "Annual Products, quantity, kind, and value" of the specified manufacturer.[220] As an asset of Southern, slave holding industries, slaves would be regarded as a major investment but with generally no earned wages.

Ironically and sadly, even in death, these slaves were not to be acknowledged as "free." Schedule 3, addressing the "Statistics of Mortality," was designed for use throughout the population of June 1, 1860. In addition to specifying the name, age, sex, and color of those deceased during the prior 12 months, "condition" was included in this moribund enumeration. Under the heading 5, entitled "Free or Slave," the space was to be left blank if the person was free and filled with letter "S" if the individual was a slave.[221] Apparently, there was no manumission for slaves even when life ceased. In addition, under *Occupation,* the deceased slave would still be identified as, "whether such slave was usually employed as a field hand, house servant, or in mechanical pursuits—the words, 'house servant,' 'field hand,' 'blacksmith,' 'carpenter,' would, in the case of slaves, indicate with sufficient clearness the nature of their previous employment."[222] The term, "employed," seems out of place for human chattel occupation. It is further defined for census reasons, as "*Profession, occupation, or trade of each person over fifteen years of age.*"[223]

---

[218] Pg 26-27, schedule No. 5

[219] http:www.geo.msu.edu/geogmich/ironsteel.html

[220] Pg 27 points 8-14

[221] Pg 20, Schedule 3, point 5.

[222] Pg 21, point 9, Census 1860

[223] Pg 15, point 10

Further specified instruction included, "In fine, record the occupation of every human being, male and female, (over 15,) who has an occupation or means of living, and let your record be so clear as to leave no doubt on the subject."[224]

As the Assistant came to the end of the engrossing forms, Schedule No. 6, rounded out "Social Statistics." Possibly to be gleaned from public records, in addition to the personal interview, value of real estate, taxes, information regarding libraries, colleges, student numbers, newspapers, magazines and churches was to be ascertained and described in remarkable detail.[225] The disappointing statistics of the 8th Census, from a southern point of view, was clearly reiterated in the impressive, "A History of American Manufactures from 1608 to 1860: Exhibiting THE ORIGIN AND GROWTH OF THE PRINCIPAL MECHANIC ARTS AND MANUFACTURES, FROM THE EARLIEST COLONIAL PERIOD TO THE ADOPTION OF THE CONSTITUTION; AND COMPRISING ANNALS OF THE INDUSTRY OF THE UNITED STATES IN MACHINERY, MANUFACTURES AND USEFUL ARTS, WITH A NOTICE OF THE IMPORTANT INVENTIONS, TARIFFS, AND THE RESULTS OF EACH DECENNIAL CENSUS." This two volume set, by J. Leander Bishop, A.M., M.D. was further entitled, "To which are added STATISTICS OF THE PRINCIPAL MANUFACTURING CENTRES, AND DESCRIPTIONS OF REMARKABLE MANUFACTORIES AT THE PRESENT TIME."[226] Of course by the time of publication of this set, with graphic details of southern deficits relative to northern industrial strengths, the Civil War was about three years old. Very interestingly, "Manufactures of the Southern States" was to be described in minutia.

In the language of the day, "When this work was projected, the plan included a detailed and minute account of the progress that had been made in establishing manufactures in the Southern States. The Hon. Jefferson Davis, then a Senator in the United States Congress, employed a gentleman in Mississippi to report upon the development of manufactures in that State; but the only report that was ever received from him was letter of inquiry. The Hon. Alexander H. Stephens addressed a letter, giving all the information that he possessed in relation to the manufactures of Georgia; which, however, was so little, that the letter is not worth publishing. Since then, there has been so much interruption in the postal arrangements, that it is difficult to communicate with these correspondents; and as several hundred thousand men, well armed (sic), have tried for three years to visit Richmond, and have not succeeded, our readers will excuse us from attempting a personal visit, and be content with the information, meager as it is, furnished in the Census returns."[227] Who would ever expect such lively and, in a sense, dark humor in such a literary source.

In addition, the documenters of the time face the same issues as do historians of today. While establishing this two volume set, published in fact by the same Northern publishing

---

[224]Pg. 15, point 10

[225]U.S. Census 1860

[226]Title page-------Edward Young & Co. 1864

[227]A History of American Manufactures, pg. 805

firm, Edward Young & Co. of Philadelphia, as a reputable resource, the writer discounts his own information. While discussing the Manufactures of Cincinnati, Ohio, "In 1859 Mr. Charles Cist published a work on 'Cincinnati as it is,' in which he stated that the manufacturing industry of that city yielded a value of $112,254,400 annually. In 1860 the same Mr. Cist was one of the Assistant Marshals for the Eighth Census, and his return and those of his associates, when added, give for the whole of Hamilton County a product of $46,691,617. We have no doubt whatever, knowing how negligent census officials are, that this return is below the truth, but we are equally confident that Cincinnati does not produce a hundred million (sic) of dollars yearly."[228]

Despite the inaccuracies of history, one paragraph reflects the truth of the era: "The South is now passing through the ordeal by fire, but will come forth, like iron from the furnace, strengthened and purified. A new, intelligent, and enterprising people will take possession of her desolated fields; and the day is not distant when many a stately edifice will be musical with the clanging of machinery and those sounds of diversified industry that quicken the pulse of Nation, and prolong the life of a Republic."[229] Well said.

Hopefully, these reflections on the antebellum and Civil War years will help to prove wrong a less familiar quote from Santayana, "only the dead have seen the end of war."[230]

THE LAST REVIEW.

Figure 117 - Last Review **Harper's pg. 772**

---

[228] A History of American Manufactures Pg. 796

[229] A History of American Manufactures, pg 809

[230] George Santayana (1922) *Soliloquies in England and Later Soliloquies*, number 25

About the Author

I am author Vernette M. Carlson, MD, a rural family practice physician in the Upper Peninsula of Michigan. I am a native Texan, and transplant to the U.P. as a child. This background led to an early appreciation for the history of Texas, the Civil War, and regional pride. In addition to avid, lifelong studying of United States history, and travel to historic sites, I have endeavored to pass this interest on to family and friends, and even to my patients. With a special love and appreciation of the Civil War era, I have chosen to reenact the role of a grieving widow of the War, sometimes as Mary Lincoln (although I am at least six inches too tall and actually too thin—at least at the time of this writing—to be physically identical). In the totally black garb of the full mourning period, full hoop skirt, bonnet with veil, gloves, purse, etc., I can gain the attention of psychiatric care-givers and most members of the lay, non-history addicted public.

This garb, also, allows me to combine my medical training with the re-enacting. I cover injuries, diseases, amputations, grieving, mourning dress, spiritual beliefs, Abraham Lincoln's mortal wound, John Wilkes Booth's spinal injury, and many other details of the mid-nineteenth century which hopefully inspire more interest in our history. In addition, our family's love of antiques has proven helpful in supplying props for these presentations. These treasures include coins from the era, Confederate currency, checks written by Robert Lincoln and his wife, also named Mary, and a genuine hand written note authored by Abraham Lincoln when he was in office.

My most devoted students include my husband, Brian M. Williams, and our four kids, Bethany, Ben, Sarah, and Noah. They have become very tolerant of travel to battlefields, museums, historic sites, and innumerable cannons. I have also encouraged their participation as re-enactors. This is a little challenging as the younger three offspring are adopted from South Korea and there was minimal Asian presence in the United States Civil War.

I have published articles in pen collecting magazines, newspapers, and in medical journals. My next book, *Preaching a Social Gospel; Eccentricities of the Shepherds,* covering colorful evangelists and preachers of the United States, is underway. I hope you enjoy this book and can share it with your friends and relatives, cultivating and preserving a deep respect for those resilient Americans, Northerners and Southerners, who endured Civil War.

PUBLISHER'S NOTE

Now that you have finished reading this book, the author would be most grateful if you would take the time to post an honest review of it on Amazon, Barnes & Noble or any other online bookseller's web site.

Anyone with an Amazon account can post reviews, even if you purchased the book somewhere else. If you ever purchased anything on Amazon, you have an account. A fair, objective and authentic review is requested so others may benefit from your opinion. It need not be long, just a couple of well chosen sentences can be enough to help potential readers decide if the book is worth their time. Your opinion is valuable to both the author and the publisher.

The author-publisher team put a lot of effort into editing the manuscript before publication, but no book is perfect. If you notice an error, you could help improve future editions by emailing us with page number and line so it can be corrected.

Finally, if you enjoyed the book, be sure to tell your friends about it, in person and on social media such as Facebook, Twitter, LinkedIn and others.

Gene D. Robinson
publisher@moonshinecovepublishing.com

CPSIA information can be obtained at www.ICGtesting.com
Printed in the USA
BVOW052157270113

311539BV00004B/19/P